MY PRAYERS, MY PURPOSE, GOD'S PROMISE:
A Collection of Prayers

Andrea L. Carson

ISBN: 9798674151142

Credits:

Publisher: TME Publishing
Photographer: TSEED Graphics
Editor: Rhonda McAlister
Cover: TME Publishing

Dedication

This book is dedicated to my late parents, Wyatt Turner and Ometris Ballew Walker. They lived a life in front of their four children that illustrated the true power of prayer and the benefits of being faithful. Through their example I became aware of the awesome power of prayer and the bountiful benefits of accepting Jesus Christ as my Savior at an early age.

I thank God for gifting me with Wyatt and Ometris as my parents. Their example of unconditional love coupled with a spirit of service has left an indelible impact on me and is truly the foundation of their legacy. They taught us to love God, love ourselves and treasure our family, values which have continued to be passed on to the next generation. I consider it a blessing to be their first-born child.

"Dad and Mom, for all your sacrifices, your love and for introducing me to my Creator, I say thank you".

~ Love, Andrea

Preface

When I think about my prayers, my purpose, and His promise it gives me great joy because at this stage of my life, I feel like I finally have things relatively altogether. Believe me, I couldn't have sat down and openly shared with you like this when I was in my 20's, 30's or early 40's. Life at that time was for living and not necessarily living in His will. After a devastating tragedy struck my family in the early 2000's, I was forced to sit still, conduct some real introspection and give God complete control of my life. It was not easy looking at me with a clear lens. Once I let go of the demons in my life and allowed the "Sonshine" to permeate my body from head to toe I was able to clearly see my purpose.

My prayers have always been the most important part of my faith walk. I can truly say I have acquired a stronger prayer life as my walk with God sifted and He became the nucleus of my being. It's my honor and a true privilege when I can simply go to God in prayer, no matter where I am, who I am with or what the situation may be.

Through this book of prayers and inspiration, I hope you can find personal insight, peace of mind and perhaps even find your way to have a closer walk with Christ. They often say prayer changes things, but I have to honestly say prayer has changed me.

ACKNOWLEDGEMENTS

Thanks to my husband Jeffrey, for his patience, his persistence, and his love. Thank you to my daughter Courtney for her gentle nudging and her constant checking to see if I was working on my prayer book. I am grateful to my youngest daughter Lauren for her supportive prayers and always telling me to stay focused.

I cannot forget to acknowledge all of the women in my life who have encouraged me and supported me while I was posting prayers on Face Book. Your encouragement led me to this literary experience. I also want to say thank you to my life-long prayer partner and sister friend, Tina for her support and prayers. Lastly, I want to thank Rhonda McAlister, for being my guiding light through this literary journey.

Thanks to everyone that has crossed my path and reminded me that I can do all things through Christ.

~Be Blessed, Andrea

TABLE OF CONTENTS

INTRODUCTION

My husband and daughters have been telling me for years to sit down and write a book. They wanted me to write about my experiences at work, but I was led to write this collection of prayers. I had to wait on God's timing, and I guess this is it. Since November of 2018, I have been writing and posting prayers on social media. I did it for me more so than anyone else because I was so tired of all the negative postings on social media.

As a child I remember going to midweek prayer meetings with my mother. I can still hear them singing "A charge to keep I have, a God to glorify, or Sweet hour of prayer, sweet hour of prayer" as we walked into the sanctuary. Watching my mother and others kneeling in front of the pew and praying was the first time I realized your attitude and the atmosphere needs to be right in order to get through to God. Through the posting of these prayers, I have grown stronger in my prayer life and I have been able to intercede on other's behalf. My one on one time with the Lord has become the fuel that keeps me moving forward. God and I commune best during the early morning hours as my husband lays there sleeping so peacefully.

It never ceases to amaze me how God gives me the right words at the right time for circumstances that I am dealing with or that might occur that day. I have learned in my faith walk what God has for me is for me and He is never late supplying my needs. While posting my prayers on social media I have been blessed to hear from others that a particular prayer blessed them or helped a loved one. I thank God that He gave me a gift which allows me to express how I feel through my writings.

I hope all who read the pages that follow will find peace, strength, joy and be inspired. Whatever help they may be looking for. As for me, I know that my prayer life has and continues to change me. My prayer life helped me find clarity in my purpose and I know that God is keeping all His promises. I stand on His promises as I walk in my purpose and elevate my prayer life. My conversations with God have covered all situations and topics and I am so grateful that God has an ear for me and has His hand on me. I love the Lord and I love my one on one time with Him.

FOREWORD

James 5:16 KJV Confess your faults one to another, and pray one for another, that ye may be healed. The effectual fervent prayer of a righteous man availeth much.

Life tends to become overwhelming and stressful. We live in a capitalistic culture where egotism and narcissism are developed and are applauded as positive traits. Such a time as this, self-involvement and self-aggrandizement rule the day. This very attitude has even crept its way into the very fabric of the Church. One of the most selfless things a Christian can do is pray.
However, many have turned prayer into a petty petitioning instead of the powerful prayer that is selfless. Through prayer, you are truly submitting to the will of God. Proper prayer relies on 3 things: the posture (humbling oneself), purpose (motive) and the person (who is praying and who they are praying too).

Deaconess Andrea Carson is a shining example of what it means to have strong prayer life. I have had the privilege of being her Pastor for the past 5 years. Through her dedicated and diligent work in the ministry, I have seen what it means to be a servant leader. I almost feel guilty for God allowing someone as Christ-centered, emotionally intelligent, caring, and committed as Deaconess

Carson into my life. I can witness and attest, that even during numerous personal trials, tragedies, and tribulations her faith and prayer life have never wavered. Andrea has exuded excellence not only in her secular career but also in her New Testament church work. I know that anyone that has the privilege to read these heartfelt prayers will be blessed by them, because they have truly been given by the Holy Spirit, cultivated by her experience, and birthed through her heart. With this book Andrea has truly accepted the calling of 1 Thessalonian 5:17 to "pray without ceasing".

Be Blessed,

Pastor Fredrick Lemons II

Chapter 1: Thank You Lord–Prayers of Gratitude

"Let them give thanks to the Lord for his unfailing love and his wonderful deeds for mankind, for he satisfies the thirsty and fills the hungry with good things". Psalm 107:8-9

When we go to God in prayer it is very important that we always acknowledge our blessings and give God the glory and show Him the honor He is due through our prayers of thanksgiving. Thankfulness and gratitude should be a constant state of being for all of us. When you stop to think about the goodness of the Lord and just look at your own individual blessings- gratitude should be an ever-present state of mind.

Dear Lord,

Thank You for being the nucleus of my life, the center of my joy and the reason I have life. Thank You for loving me even in my messiness and dysfunction. Saying thank You sounds so shallow sometimes, but I do thank You for all things, everything and more.

Lord I come as humbly as I can to say that my heart is full of gratitude and I can't find enough ways to say THANK YOU. Thank You for the small things, the harm You kept me from, the air which expands my lungs. Thank You Lord.

Thank You for salvation, for redemption and for

favor. Thank You for forgiveness and for second chances. Thank You for being the great I am.

In Jesus Name, Amen

***"The Lord is my shepherd; I shall not want." –
Psalm 23:1***

Somedays we wake up and just wonder how we continue to survive through all the mayhem and chaos around us. We serve a God who is merciful and who never leaves His children alone. As every good shepherd knows you must know your sheep and keep watch over them. Aren't we blessed to have the ultimate Shepherd in Jesus?

Dear Lord,
Thank You for Your abundant blessings and for giving us life! Thank You for Your grace and mercy which allows us to still be here. Thank You for this time in our life where we are walking with you, living because of You, and striving to be closer to You.

Lord, thank You for the challenges and life altering experiences as they have caused us to be reminded of the fact that You are in control of all things. Forgive us for complaining or pouting when we thought things should have gone differently. Help us to be more appreciative of Your grace and mercy that continues to keep us covered.

Thank You for our overflow and for us being able to realize what You have for us is more than enough. We clearly understand what it means when it's said little becomes much when you place it in the master's hands.

Every time, we thought we were at the end of something or in need of something, You supplied our needs. Your grace, Your mercy and Your love have no limits and for that we are so grateful. Thank You Lord, yes, we are extremely grateful!!In Jesus name, Amen

I will give thanks to you Lord with my whole heart- Psalm 9:1

Dear Lord,

We say thank You Lord for always making a way for us. There is no greater way maker, deal broker, trouble shooter or problem solver than You.

Thank You for being a true Shepherd of Your flock. Making sure we don't have to want for any of our needs or beg for any of the desires of our hearts. Thank You for leading and guiding us along the way so we don't stray far from You. Thank You for restoration and for reviving of our spirits.

Lord, we thank You for moving mountains and sustaining us in our valley experiences. You are our Shepherd; our Way maker and we are so grateful. We appreciate the table You have prepared for us even in the midst of all the naysayers and haters. Thank You for this table spread with love, understanding, patience, knowledge, and kindness.

Lastly, we say thank You for allowing goodness

and mercy to follow us all the days of our
appointed time. Yes, You are our Shepherd and
we shall not want In Jesus' name, Amen

**I am crucified with Christ; and it is no longer I who
live, but it is Christ who lives in me. Galatians 2:20**

Dear Lord,

It's me again just being grateful that You never get
tired of hearing from me or any of your children. I
am so blessed to be able to live my life out loud and
on purpose.

 I want to say thank You for dying on that cross in
my place; and thank You for raising from the dead
and leaving me a comforter so I can live and love on
purpose. Your love for me and the world is simply
indescribable, but I thank God for it! Because of
Your sacrifice I am not afraid to live a life where
others can see that I love the Lord. Dear Lord, help
me and all of Your children to remember, we aren't
ashamed of the good news of Jesus and we stand
firmly rooted on Your Word.

Thanking You for the burning passion I have to live
on purpose while serving my purpose. Grateful for
Your guiding light which directs my path and causes
me to stay focused even when I have become my
greatest distraction. Lord, I want to live for You, live
a life that not only pleasing in Your sight but one that
is fruitful and rewarding.

Thank you for allowing me to breathe, move and have my mind so I can continue to live and love on purpose while living out loud and fine tuning the purpose You created in me.

In Jesus' name, Amen

How precious is your steadfast love, O God!

Psalm 36:7a

Dear Lord,

Here I am with You in the early morning hours, just me and You with our one on one time. Thank you for our time and for being available whenever I call. I say Thank you Lord. Thank you, Lord, for loving us without reservation or judgment. Your love engulfs us and provides a warm and safe haven for us, we say Thank you.

When we are disobedient, stubborn or in our "know everything" mode You still love us, and You still allow us to feel Your warmth and presence. Thank You! Lord, Your love for us is so amazing that words can't describe it! You died so we could live, You forgive us over and over again and You never leave or abandon us. Your love is the best gift and greatest thing which ever happened to us and we are so very so grateful!

Because of Your love for us, we can't help but love you!! Loving You is so easy as we never have to be concerned about You failing, forsaking, or hurting us. How exciting it is to love You and know that falling in love with Jesus is indeed the best thing that ever happened to and for us. Yes falling in love with You enriches us, because You loved us first, You sacrificed for us, You created us, You provide for us, You forgive us and did we mention You loved us first!! Yes, Jesus loves us this we know and Lord we love You too!! Oh, how we love Jesus!

Thanking You in advance for everything!

Amen.

But seek ye first his kingdom and his righteousness, and all these things will be given to you as well."- Matthew 6:33

*Dear Lord,
I used to panic and get frustrated when I would struggle with insomnia. That was before I realized these hours are our one on one, "Alone Time" with each other. Lord, I thank You for these times when You step in and speak to me. You give me clarity and often times You lay out the road map for the next challenges I have to maneuver or path You want me to take. Lord, Thank You for whispering to my heart and speaking out loud to my head; helping me to move with logical and prayerful precision while executing all my moves with love and respect.*

I am grateful to You Lord for the Alone Time as that is truly when you replenish me, refresh me, and restore me to a higher place in You. I love my Alone Time with You Jesus, as these times are when I clearly hear You guiding me, I feel You

*invigorating my spirit and I sense Your presence
which gives me peace, joy and a zeal to honor
You. Thank You for keeping me up so we can
have our time of meditation, reflection, and review.
Thank You Lord, for speaking to me, guiding me
and above all else, loving me. Insomnia is not a
problem for me, it's my opportunity to commune
and communicate with my Creator, my Savior,
and my Friend. What a friend I have in Jesus. I am
so thankful for You and all You have done.
Thankful for my alone time with You.*

In Jesus Name,

Amen

I will give thanks to the Lord, because of his righteousness-Psalm 7:17

Dear Lord,

Saying thank You oftentimes does not sound adequate enough to express my true spirit of gratefulness. You are my all and all, my beginning and ending. I say thank You Lord, for keeping me when I cannot keep myself. Thank You for fixing my situations when they are out of my control and for giving me another chance.

I thank You and I reverence You for being God all by yourself. Today, I just stopped by to say thank You for keeping me and knowing what I need when I need it.

In Jesus' name, Amen

"In their heart's humans plan their course, but the LORD establishes their steps."
- Proverbs 16:9

Once you suffer a traumatic event in your life you are prone to struggle with post-traumatic stress disorder. Whenever I am driving and enter a construction zone my heart pounds and my hands fiercely grip the wheel. I get the same way whenever I hear or see a medical rescue helicopter. It took me three years of therapy and hundreds of nerve pills before I realized my answer laid in my faith. I stopped asking God for anything and I simply started thanking Him for everything. After all I had been through, I was still standing and able to call upon His name whenever I needed to.

Dear Lord,

Lord, I thank God I am still here! Many are not getting up today as their time on this side expired. Lord, thank You for giving me one more chance to get things together. I am very grateful, for truly I am unworthy of Your blessings upon me. Thank You Lord.

Lord sometimes we feel physically and emotionally drained this morning, but even in our tired state we find the strength to say "Thank You "and we have peace of mind even in our tired state.

Yes, Lord, we still give You all the honor and all the praise! Thank You for not only loving us, but for loving us when we are unlovable, disobedient, and out of order. To think that You took time to divinely create us in Your image and to give up Your life so we might live... how could we ever be ungrateful or out of order? Thank You!! Lord, our eyes swell up with tears when we think of all the "could have beens or should have beens". You have kept us and been beyond good to us, in spite of all we have thought, done, or said!! We have unspeakable joy when we think of You and all You have kept us from and brought us through.

We are by no means perfect, but we thank You for allowing us to feel Your perfect presence and perfect peace in our lives! Yes, thank You for this day. We thank You for being our Lord and Savior! Our Help and our Hope! Our Shelter and our Source! Our Go To and Our Get Through! Our Protector and Provider! Thank You for being our Joy and our Justification and yes, Lord, thank You for being our All in All and the Answer for all our concerns! Thank You for being our Everything and for giving us a chance to have Everlasting life!! Oh, how we thank You for Saving us from ourselves and for Showering us with blessings. Lord, we thank You for our life, Your love for us and Your listening ear! We Love You Lord! Thank You for this moment and our time with You!!
Amen

Teach me to do Your will, for You are my God; Let Your good spirit lead me on level ground- Psalm 143:10

Good Morning Lord,
I come this morning to say thank You! Thank You for revealing to me Your desires for my life. Thank You for guiding me and leading me so I might walk in the right direction and I would always focus on You and Your Word.

I get so excited when I think on all the blessings You keep showering me and my loved ones with. Just this month alone You have kept the floods, tornadoes, and other storms from harming us. You have provided all the means we needed to have adequate shelter and food. Lord, I thank You!! It's Your Word that convicts me and causes me to turn in the right direction. I am so grateful for Your example of love which always serves as my example of how to love and cherish my beloved family and friends. It serves as an even greater guide in reminding me how to love those who are often times unlovable, thank You!!!

I am so overwhelmed when I think on all the goodness and love You have shown me! You kept me though my darkest times when I was widowed, alone and in a very scary place. Lord, for that I will forever sing Your praises! Thank You for always giving me the words I need to talk with You each day and yes Lord thank You for every answered prayer.

On this beautiful day, I say thank You for giving me the patience and foresight I need to live peacefully and to have unspeakable joy while chaos might be all

around me!
I praise You for the wonderful gift of life You have
given me. Yes, today it's all about being thankful for
Your goodness to me! I love You Lord
In Jesus Name,
Amen

"Wait patiently for the LORD. Be brave and courageous. Yes, wait patiently for the LORD." – Psalm 27:14

He's an on Time God

For nearly 5 years I prayed for a promotion on my job. I worked harder than many and played by all the rules. I sat at my job and watched people with less experience and less education become promoted and some even become my supervisors. Finally, one day I asked my mentor, what am I doing wrong? I wasn't doing anything wrong; it just wasn't my turn. Wow did that sting. At the age of 38, I saw God not only open doors for me, but He opened a door that I didn't even know existed. I went from a being line staff to an administrator without even applying for the job. My God opened my door. He can and will do the same for you. His timing is perfect. I was and I remain so grateful for
God opening doors and, in some cases, keeping the wrong door closed.

Good Morning Lord,
Just stopping by to say thank You! Thank You for all the doors you have opened for us. Lord forgive us for taking for granted the small things that You provide each day! Thank You, for opening doors of opportunity so we can provide for ourselves and our families. Lord, thank You for opening doors of healing where we had been struggling with physical and emotional illness.

Lord, we say thank You for opening doors where we

found compassion and love on the other side! As we navigate our way through the various hallways and walkways of life, we say Thank You for all the open doors and for the direction and guidance You have given us to walk through the right door! Lord as we prepare to seize this day, we also want to say

Thank You for the doors which You kept closed. Doors that could have led to destruction, decay, and death!   Yes Lord, we Thank You for all the doors and for the ability to receive the blessings connected to them.

In Jesus Name, Amen.

"Let everything that hath breath praise the LORD. Praise ye the LORD."- Psalm 150:6

REFLECTION

What are somethings you are grateful for?

____

____

____

What are some of the things you have taken (or still take) for granted?

____

____

____

How have you shown others the importance of being grateful?

____

____

____

REFLECTION

Can you identify a situation where God kept a door closed for your greater good?

____

____

____

____

____

____

____

How did you respond when a door you thought had been closed was opened for you?

____

____

____

____

____

REFLECTION

Why do you think it is so difficult for you to wait on God to move on your behalf?

____

____

____

____

____

____

____

____

Can you list a few times where you interfered with God's timing in your life?

1.

2.

3.

4.

"My times are in Your hand."- Psalm 31:15

Dear Lord,

Thank you for keeping us during the night to rise early today to be able to say Thank You Lord!!! Thank you for being an on-time God. Answering our pleas and prayers when You know we were ready to handle the answer. Showing up to rescue us from ourselves right in the moment when we are about to cross over an un-crossable line.   Providing the way or resource we needed just when we have run out of options!   Yes, we come to say Thank you Lord for being that on-time God.   Thank you for being my life saver, my safety net and yes, my life support! Your time is always on time and in time… Thank You!!! Thank you for showing us that You always are there when needed the most. You never leave your children alone. Happy to have an on-time Savior!

In Jesus Name, Amen.

"Create in me a pure heart, O God, and renew a steadfast spirit within me."
– Psalm 51:10

Dear Lord,

It's another beautiful morning and I am so glad about it. Lord, we are so grateful for all Your goodness shown toward us and the blessings you have bestowed upon us. Today, we come to thank You for the shift in our atmosphere and the increase You are bringing to our lives. Increase in our faith, our love, our wisdom, and our understanding. We thank You for the pruning and weeding You have done in our lives.

Lord, those friends and family members who were smothering us with their negative vibes and energy, thank You for gently pushing us out of their path. Lord, that unmanageable problem that keeps us up and crying at night, thank You for the shift in our thinking. It caused us to be reminded that You are in control and what we bring to You to fix, we need to leave it alone once we give it to You. Lord, thank You for the plans You have for us and the truths You have been showing us.

We love You Lord and we honor You. It is a privilege just to be able to call upon your name. We realize it has nothing to do with us, but it is all about You. We will remain faithful and dedicated to Your Word, Your will, and Your promises. We are grateful that You lifted us to a new place in You. Thank You for shifting us to a higher level of praise and a more spiritual mode of communing with You.

We thank You for the blessing of being able to recognize that we are being shifted to a closer walk with You. As we walk in our purpose let us do so with passion, persistent prayer, and a powerful promise to always be in Your will. Thank You for our shift, our elevation, and our closer walk with Thee.

In Jesus Name, **Amen.**

Devote yourselves to prayer being watchful

and thankful-Colossians 4:2

Dear Lord,

I woke up this morning and I was still here! Our

family members all intact and up and about their

day! The sky was still it's majestic blue with rolling

fluffy clouds with a few dark clouds filled with rain

slowly approaching.

Our lungs expanded and we exhaled, while our

legs kept us standing without buckling. Our arms

were able to be raised and mouth opened letting

words flow right out. Our eyes were opened to see

just how great our God is.

Lord, thank You for all You stopped from

happening that would have harmed or hurt us!

Thank You for surrounding us with people who

love us and who love You!

Then sings my soul my Savior God to Thee!! How

great Thou Art! How Great Thy Art!

Thanking You for being You.

In Jesus Name,

Amen

Dear Lord,

As we reflect on this beautiful morning about Your goodness and grace, we can't help but feel an overwhelming sense of generosity. Nobody knows us better than You. Nobody knows are sins, our flaws, and our shortcomings like You do. We are abundantly blessed, because no one knows our heart and our true desires other than You. Your grace and Your mercy have and continue to follow us all the days of our lives.

Sitting here thinking and thanking about God's Grace- the freely given, undeserved favor and love of our God. Through Your grace, You keep blessing us in spite of the fact that we are so unworthy and undeserving. Grace, Your extended goodness to us even in our times of ungodliness. Thank You. Grace, God's grace is so sufficient for me and you. Through Your grace we also reap the benefits of second and third chances, opportunities to show You we appreciate and respect the favor You have given to us.

Grace, goodness, grace.....amazing grace, God given grace, the undeniable goodness of the Lord.....thank You God. Grace! Your amazing grace, greater than all my sins, grace, the chain breaker, Your grace gives us liberty and Your grace is not only sufficient for us, it's unmatched, it's larger and more massive than any of our transgressions and it is free! Amazing, wonderful, unmerited, unexplainable, and so underserved is this grace You keep giving to us. Thank You for grace, for favor and for being the God of our lives who loves us and keeps us!!

*Amazing Grace how sweet the sound that saved a
wretch like me. I once was lost but now, I am found. I
was blind but now I can see. Grace....thank you
Jesus! Grace......Thank You Lord!!*
In Jesus Name, Amen
Hello Lord,
*As I woke up this morning all I could think about was
Your loving kindness towards us! Thank You Lord.*

*Lord, thank You for forgiving us and loving us in a
way that only You can. Lord, thank You for Your
patience with s as we continue to navigate this thing
called life. Thank You for helping us to understand
that following You is the answer, and everything will
fall into place.*

*Thank You for Your Word and Your Way is what
enables us to love ourselves and be those vessels of
love, kindness, truth and peace that you created and
commanded us to be.*
*Thank You for one more chance to serve You, live for
You and spread the good news about You to others.*
In Jesus Name

Chapter 2: Something Happens When Women Pray-Prayers for Women

Charm is deceitful, and beauty is vain, but a woman who fears the Lord is to be praised". - Proverbs 31:20

It is difficult having to maneuver being a woman in today's world. We have to wear so many hats, at times we get overwhelmed and even exhausted. It is vital to have an anchor that holds us steady and keeps us afloat.

I have found along this life's journey that my faith and my relationship with Christ have been that anchor that holds me down. I find solace and comfort in knowing once I have prayed and left whatever the daily challenge was in His hands, I can make my way forward.

As women we need to be more dedicated to self-care and loving ourselves without restriction. This chapter of prayers is for all the women out there who make sacrifices for others, who stand in the gap for their sisters and who carry the title of mom, mother, granny, caregiver, sis, Sista girl and girlfriend. No matter how much we have to do or how much we are forced to carry, we have an anchor in Jesus, a comforter in Him and He loves us without restraint or condition.

Therefore encourage one another and build one another up, just as you are doing. -1 Thessalonians 5:11

Good Morning Lord,
It's another day's journey, and I am so glad about it,
so glad to still be above the ground. Thank You Lord.

As women we sometimes wear a mask and it can be for so many different reasons. Some wear one to hide one to hide their pain, others their insecurities and others wear a mask to keep people from getting close to the person behind that mask.

Lord, we come right now asking You to help us so we can appreciate our real beauty, our natural selves and help us to accept ourselves for the divine creation we are. Lord, remind us that You blew breath into Adam and You pulled us from Adams rib. Help us to always be mindful that anything and everything created by You is all good.

Empty the pockets of low self-esteem and unworthiness we carry around and fill them up with self-love and self-worth. Open our eyes so we can see our inner beauty and inner strength. Lord, remove the feelings of not being good enough, not being pretty enough and not being thin enough and give us the courage and boldness we need to realize we are beautiful, we are strong and what we think matters.

We thank You for Your Word which reminds us that we are divine creatures. It reassures us that it is what we think, speak, and believe which makes us beautiful, lovable, and loving. Lord, help us to stand firmly on Your promises, which we know never sway or fail. Please, help us to dig deep into our souls so we can be brave like Esther, be filled with hope like Hannah, be compassionate and loving like Ruth and be obedient like Mary. Give us the inner strength and self-love we need to see our beauty and realize we don't have to wear a mask to make to fit in.

Thank You for creating us in Your divine, delightful and delicate image. We love You Lord for giving us eyes that can foresee a vision, ears that can hear Your commands, a tongue which can speak life and spread love and a heart which beats to God's righteous rhythm keeping us in step with Your will. Thank You for removing our mask and replacing it with a smile which displays Your love, a glow which come from communing with You and a tame tongue which speaks power and life not pity and pain.

We love You Lord; therefore it is easy to love ourselves. We treasure You Lord; therefore, it is easy to see our self-worth and we praise and thank You Lord, therefore it is easy to put our trust in You Lord. Thank You for giving us the inner strength to stop wearing our mask. Thank You for equipping us so we can walk boldly and live our lives knowing that we are divine, we are inspired, and we are Yours.

In Jesus Name, Amen

"She opens her mouth with wisdom and the teachings of kindness are on her tongue"- Proverbs31:26

Good Morning Lord!
We come today asking for a covering and protection over all mothers. Lord, we are standing in the gap for those moms who are dealing with depression, worry or anxiety. Lord replace their anxiousness with the ability to trust You, deflate their depression and replace it with delight in knowing they can conquer ALL things through You.

We come asking for strength for the moms that are weary from all their responsibilities in keeping their family intact. Lord, prop them up on every leaning side and let them realize its ok to lean on You!

Lord, please keep all mothers wrapped up in Your loving kindness. Let them be able to find time to refuel and refresh. We know You rested on the 7th day, so moms need to rest too!

Lord, give mothers wisdom so they can impart it into those who cross their paths. Thank You for all of the praying mothers and the tears they shed while keeping us covered in prayer!

Teach us as moms how to truly let go and let God! Please booster our resolve as we are always reminded You are in control of every situation.

Lord, please let mothers circle around each other giving them positive encouragement, becoming each other's source of inspiration and support. Give mothers the patience they need to be still and wait on

You.

Lastly Lord, we want to say thank You Lord for all you have already done for all of the mothers in the land. Thank You for being an all knowing, all seeing and all wise God who never fails His children. Thank You for Your example of love and sacrifice as it is road map for all mothers.

Lord, thank You for motherhood, mothers, moms and all those in a nurturing motherly capacity (i.e. aunts, grandma's, god mothers and foster moms).
In Jesus Name,
Amen

She is clothed in strength and dignity and she laughs without fear of the future-Proverbs 31:25

Dear Father,

Thank you for the opportunity to be able to have this one on one time with you. Lord, today I come asking covering for the women in this land. Help women of all colors, shapes, sizes, and political persuasions to realize their collective power. Lord, spark the fire of Ruth like love in their hearts so they will be sincere and dedicated friends. Give them the spirit of Phoebe, so they will willingly serve those who can't help themselves.

Lord give them a sense of power and authority over their lives, so they won't be subjected to abuse or control from anything. Let them have a zeal to love, nurture and share their knowledge with other women and make this world a better place. Lord, let them realize it's easier and more productive to lift each other up, versus taking each other down or out.

I am praying right now Lord for an infectious and contagious move of love, respect, and harmony to begin with women of God across this land, helping to make this world a better place. We know something happens when women pray Lord show up and show us what happens when women of God lift each other up!

In Jesus Name,

Amen.

REFLECTION

Which of my friendships are healthy? What makes it a healthy relationship?

____

____

____

____

____

____

____

____

____

____

____

So do not throw away your confidence: it will be richly rewarded. You need to persevere so that when you have done the will of God, you will receive what he has promised. Hebrews 10:35-36

Hello Lord,

Thank you for waking me up in my right mind and able to see, speak, hear, and move. Today I come Lord to ask You for an increase in my resolve and my will power so that I can continue to be obedient to Your will and Your way.

Lord, help us as women to love and nurture ourselves more and to realize that we need to take time to love ourselves as we love and care for others. Help us to understand that our sacrifices for our children should not become roadblocks for us and we should make sure our children realize and see that loving yourself is important. As our hearts are filled with love for You, Lord help us to love ourselves completely and without reservation. Realizing as we love ourselves our ability to nurture and care for others is elevated to a new place.

Thank you, Lord, for releasing me and other women from the bondage of low self-esteem, self-sacrifice and always putting ourselves last. Thank you for helping us to realize it is okay to love ourselves unconditionally. Thank you for loving us and giving us the resolve to love ourselves out loud and on purpose! I love you Lord and I am so glad I learned to truly love me!
In Jesus Name,
Amen

**Don't you know that your body is a temple of the Holy Spirit who is in you, whom you have from God and that you are not your own.
1 Corinthians 6:19Set**

Dear Lord,

Today we come with a very unique request, but we already know, nothing is too hard for our God. Lord, as women we worry about our weight and our appearance. Many of us have regular exercise routines. Right now, Lord we are asking for help with our workout and exercise routines.

Lord, help us so we can do our sit-ups increasing our ability to carry a heavier load when needed. Help us to muster enough strength to run a marathon versus a relay, because we know the race isn't given to the swift, but to the one who endures to the end.

Help us with our squats, so we can have strong legs to stand firm on your Word. Please, support our backs as we do these push-ups to ensure our arms are strong enough to carry any load we are given, and our knees are sturdy enough, so they won't bend unless in prayer. Lord, increase our levels of endurance and will power so we sprint walk through our storms, stroll in our victories and run to get our rewards. Thank You for giving us the strength and desire to elevate our workout and exercise routines as we grow in our relationship with You.
In Jesus Name, Amen

Be completely humble and gentle; be patient, bearing with one another in love. Make every effort to keep the unity of the Spirit through the bond of peace. Ephesians 4:2-3

Dear Lord,

Today I am coming on behalf of all the women who are married. I humbly come today asking that You will renew flames of love, compassion, and passion in marriages of those who have lost some of their fire. We come praying for the restoration of open and clear communication between the spouses.

Lord we come thanking You for those husbands who are a covenant partner and covering for their wife. Give those men the strength and foresight they need to continue being the heads of their households and the leader in their relationship with You showing all how important it is to walk with the Lord. Dear Lord, reinvigorate us as wives so we will always be supportive, compassionate, and nurturing in our marriage and providing a safe haven for our husbands where they can relax and let go of all the world's woes.

Thank you, Lord, for the marriage unit and for sending us our mates; for grooming us to perfectly fit each other through the good and the bad. Lord, thank you for my husband and all he does for me. From loving me, providing for me, protecting me, and praying for me. Today we ask for a renewed spirit of love, a revived spirit of unity and a refreshed spirit of patience in marriages across this land. Thanking you in advance. In Jesus Name, Amen.

Set your minds on things that are above, not on things that are on earth.
Colossians 3:2

Dear Lord,
As women we carry so many other people's loads. We step up and step in to assist and help in so many different types of situations and circumstances. Today we are asking for a clear focus. Lord. Open our eyes so we can clearly see what You have in store for us and not let our vision become blurred by worldly lusts.

Lord, we have so many different people pulling on us for this and for that. Our children need nurturing, our spouses need attention, our jobs have demands on us and we are just pulled in so many directions. Please dear Lord, revive our spirits. Give us a renewed sense of energy so we can maintain the demands of this life.

Lord help us so we will not get caught up in any man-made mess, daytime drama, fraudulent feuds, or senseless situations. Lord, please order our steps and keep us walking in an upright and wholesome manner. Give us the stamina we need to fight a good and loving fight to help our loved ones and friends who are in need.

Thank You for creating me and molding me as a woman. Please lead me and guide me as I sow into the lives of those I love and care for. As a woman I say thank You for Your loving kindness, for my God-centered relationships, family bonds and special alliances.
In Jesus Name, Amen

Do not worry about anything; instead, pray about everything. Philippians 4:6
Single Mother's Prayer

Dear Lord
Lord, first I want to thank You for allowing me to be able to bear this beautiful child of mine. Sometimes the load does get heavy as a single mother, but I would not trade it for anything. I realize that children are indeed a special gift from God and for that I say thank You Lord.

Lord, help me as a single mother to lay the correct foundation for my children. Let it be fortified in prayer, surrounded in love, and layered with understanding. Please give me the wisdom and foresight I need to make the correct decisions and chart the best path for my family. Lord, protect us from hurt, harm and danger and give me the ability to be able to provide for and protect me
family.

Please keep me in Your will and Your way so I can be a living example of Your love, Your goodness and grace. Lord, as I strive to live a life that is pleasing in Your sight, help me to show love and sow seeds of compassion, understanding and truth for my children. Let me be able to instill in them the values which will help them be their best selves.

I love You Lord and I thank You for seeing fit to allow me to be a mother. It has been my greatest joy and all I can say is thank You Lord.
In Jesus Name, Amen

**There is gold and abundance of costly stones, but the lips of knowledge are a precious jewel.
Proverbs 20:15**

Good Morning Lord,
Thank You for this sunshine kissed morning. Thank You for touching us with Your finger of love and allowing us to see this morning.
Lord, today we want to thank You for our healthy relationships. Thank You for the people You place in our lives and along our journey who give us wise counsel and sound advice. Lord, thank You for the godly and spirit filled people You send to us through various life lessons and situations. Sometimes we become stubborn or just caught up in our own challenges and mess and we need a lifesaver in human form to help get us through.

Thank You for the women You have placed in my life that help me through their prayers, their truthful conversations and their god sent correction. Thank You for the healthy relationships I have with my husband, my children and grands as a result of having examples of loving and healthy relationships from my parents.
Lord, thank You for creating us so we would need to rely and interact with one another and yes especially with You!

While our earthly relationships are important, our relationship with You is the ultimate guide and focus of our lives! Thank You for loving us in spite of our flaws, for keeping us covered regardless of our situation and for rescuing us when we aren't deserving! Thank You for showing as women of God,

that a relationship is based on love, sacrifice, and obedience.
We love You Lord! We thank You for all of the healthy and lasting relationships we have and for those that lie ahead in our future. We are blessed and better people because of our interactions with those who have sown into our lives!
In Jesus Name, Amen

Do not grieve for the joy of the Lord is your strength- Nehemiah 8:10And I am sure of this, that he who began a good work in you will bring it to completion at the day of Jesus Christ- Philippians 1:6

Dear Lord,
Thank You for allowing us to see a brand-new day. Today, we come to You knowing we are blessed, yet feeling a little low. We aren't depressed or stressed we just feel a little empty and are in need of an energy recharge. Sometimes as women we try to carry everyone's burdens, fix everyone's problems even when we know better.

Lord, every day we find ourselves dealing with challenges. Oftentimes they begin to wear on us and sometimes we take on the hurt, heartache, and hardships of those we love and care about. This can lead to us feeling empty, rundown, and even frustrated.

Today we come asking for a boost in our spiritual strength, a resurrection of our Christian resolve and a deeper connection to You, our ultimate energy source. Lord, where there is emptiness in our spirit, replace it with fullness in our hearts so our souls will feel satisfied. When we are feeling rundown and upset, replenish our energy levels so we can exercise our faith and run on a little while longer. As frustration begins to creep into the atmosphere, replace it with patience, understanding and hope.

Help us to remain steadfast and connected to You, through our prayers and our praise. Turn our weariness into welcomed expressions of genuine love for one another and for helping someone. Remove the emptiness from our hearts so we can revive ourselves and reignite the spark in our eyes and the pep in our step. Lord, turn our frustration into hope and our despair into divine fellowship with you. Pick us up from our low place and restore us to a higher elevation where we can praise and bless Your Name.

Thank You for our energy boost and our realignment in Your will. We love You because You first loved us, we honor You for Your majestic authority and we trust You because there is no greater foundation to stand on.
Thank You for all You have done and will do. In Jesus Name-we Pray, Amen.

REFLECTION

List some of the barriers that prohibited you from completely loving yourself. List how you overcame them?

But sanctify the Lord God in your hearts; and be ready always to give an answer to every man that asked you a reason of the hope that is in you with meekness and fear. 1Peter 3:15

Here I am Lord,
Thankful for another night You kept me and another morning You have allowed me to see.

Today I come asking that You will elevate our hearing as mothers, wives, and sisters into listening. Help us so we can truly listen to those who come to us in distress or just in need of an ear to pour their concerns or sorrows into. Help us Lord so we won't judge, so we won't turn off and so we won't rebuke whoever it is that needs a true listening ear.

Lord, we realize listening requires discernment, patience, and compassion, please help us to be able to show compassion while discerning the real message through patiently and actively listening to whomever needs our listening ear. Thank You for elevating our levels of hearing into levels of compassionate listening.

As today I pray Lord, I also ask that You continue to speak to our hearts. We are listening God and we are being obedient to Your desire and call over our lives. Thank You and please help us to always be a listener and not just a hearer. Let our listening motivate us

into acting or performing an action which will help the person we were listening to. Thanking You in advance for clearing our ears, connecting our ears to our hearts so we can listen with concern and respond with compassion.
In Jesus Name, Amen

REFLECTION

When was the last time you really listened to someone who is struggling with an issue without judgment or fear?

____
____
____
____
____
____
____
____
____

How did you actively let the person know you were really listening with an empathetic ear?

____
____
____
____
____

For the Lord gives wisdom; from his mouth come knowledge and understanding. Proverbs 2:6

Dear Lord,
As a woman in this world there are days life seems so unfair, so cruel and too unbelievable. We have to work harder, stay pretty, and jump through so many hoops just to arrive in this male oriented world. Lord, today we come as women first thanking You for Your grace and mercy which falls on us like fresh morning dew.

Lord, we need wisdom so when we make choices, they will be fruitful for us and our families. Lord, we need discernment, so we won't be lured by the wilds of the world and the lust of the greedy. Please grant us peace and contentment, so we will be able maneuver our way through chaos and confusion by totally depending on You. Lord we want to be available to be used by You so we can help other women who might be struggling with this journey called life.

Thank You for strong examples of womanhood and thank You for giving us the tools we need to be strong, compassion and service oriented. Give us a burst of energy when we feel weary, grant us a moment of quiet when the clatter gets too loud and Lord, give us hearts of compassion so we can care for and love those in need.

As a woman we have many mountains to climb, but we can make it because we have You on our side, Thanking You in advance for every blessing.
In Jesus Name, Amen

Therefore, I tell you that whatever you ask in prayer, believe that you have received it, and it shall be yours. -Mark 11:24

Dear Heavenly Father,
Here I am, your precious child calling on You one more time! Lord, You already know my story, my needs, my wants and yes, You even know those things I think on which aren't good for me. After all, You created me in Your divine and majestic image. You and You alone know everything about me!

Today, I come asking for a boost of energy, a renewed and revived spirit so I can be about this thing called life! Help me so I don't get caught up in any man-made mess, daytime drama, fraudulent feuds, or senseless situations! Lord direct my thoughts so they will be pure and pleasing to You. Order and guide my steps so I will walk in a just and upright way living my best life while obeying Your word and living in Your will. Give me the daily stamina I need to fight a good and loving fight, live a full and fruitful life, and stay focused on right not wrong! Lord let my light shine as I live my life and let me be humble while serving You and giving You my best!

Thank You for this thing called life! I am truly living in my overflow! Not because of material gain, but because of my healthy, happy and God centered relationships and family bonds. I am beyond grateful for Your loving kindness towards me and my family! Your arms of protection, provision and promise continue to keep me and mine and for that all I can say is Thank You!!

Lord, as I close my prayer this morning I want to say I

truly know what it means to be able to say "It is Well, It is Well With My Soul and I am So Satisfied"! Thanking You right now Lord because no matter what I am going through or facing, I can do it with You as the nucleus of my life. I am resting and leaning on You, for truly it is well with my soul!
In Jesus Name,
Amen

The wicked flee when no one pursues, but the righteous are bold as a lion-Proverbs 28:1

Dear Lord,
What a beautiful morning! Thank You Lord!
Today, we come asking for a voice! Lord give us the right words and the right timing so we can speak for the helpless and hopeless. Place a boldness and a burning desire in us as women so we will speak out against the injustices against children being held in detention centers, children being killed in our neighborhoods, children being used in human trafficking and children who are cast aside as unwanted. Help us to use our voice to cry out for these children loud and strong to get the attention of those in charge because change MUST come. Lord, give us the words that will turn to action and get things right in America! Lord instill in us the passion we need to provoke the powers that be to stop placing hurdles in the way of help and start helping these children leapfrog the hurdles. Let us as women who proclaim You as our Lord be persistent in our prayers for strength to speak boldly until change really comes. Give us the words that will start to turn hardened hearts, open closed ears, motivate compassionate souls and push people into positive action to save our children. Love is the key, so Lord give us the words and a voice to speak love, sow love and entertain love wherever it appears.
As Jesus welcomed the little children to come to Him, how can we not do the same?
Lord give us the words and a voice to speak up and speak out! Change starts with words which lead to action. Give us our voice!!
In Jesus Name, Amen

For it was the Lord your God, who rescued you from the land of Egypt. Open your mouth wide and I will fill it with the good things- Psalm 81:10

Good Morning Lord,
I say thank You for waking me up one more time.
Your grace and Your mercy continue to keep me.
Right now I come asking You to fill my me up Lord. I feel drained and somewhat sluggish from all of life's occurrences. Lord, please "Fill Me Up".
Lord remove my selfish wants and desires and replace them with what You know is best for me.
In order to be filled with You and by You, I am asking to be emptied of me. Get me out of my own way, right now in Jesus Name.
Fill me with Your love, one which is unconditional, unyielding, and uncompromising. Please pour Your fresh anointing of honesty, integrity, and truth into me Lord. Fill me up with compassion, concern, and care. Take out of me the need to be seen and instead let others see the Christ in me.
Oh Lord, fill me with a humble, patient and understanding spirit. Empty me of all bitterness and pettiness. Pour into me a vibrant spirit of joy, a strong spirit of obedience to Your Word, and a committed sense of dedication to Your Will.
Empty me of me and fill me with Your presence and Your power.
Fill me up Lord, let me be filled with You, filled by You and always feel You in my life.
Fill me up Lord.
In the Wonderful Name of Jesus, Amen

And that ye study to be quiet, and to do your own business, and to work with your own hands, as we commanded you-1Thessalonians 4:11

Good Morning Lord,
It's another morning that I am here to see, and I am so glad about it!
Lord, today we come asking for divine deliverance from the things we are doing to destroy ourselves.

First, we come asking that You would deliver us from negative self-talk. Help us to be strong enough to speak affirmative and life-giving words to ourselves. Stop the self-loathing, self-deprecating and unworthy self-talk. Let us as women replace those thoughts and words with what You have created us to be; strong, caring, praying, and nurturing women of God.

Deliver us from unhealthy one-sided relationships. Give us the insight and foresight we need to be able to properly assess people's motives and intent. Deliver us from draining, drama filled and depressing people who want to pollute our atmosphere with toxins. Help us so we value ourselves enough not to be crippled by other vulnerabilities and low self-esteem. Lord, please deliver us from staying in situations which bring us into harm's way.

Free our minds of self-destructive thoughts, loose our spirits of carrying everyone else's sorrows and deliver our hearts from holding on to the pains of our past. Deliver us from our own negative self-image. Help us to remember daily we are created in Your image and You do all things well. Please Lord deliver us from our

own negative self-talk, self-pity, and self-destructive ways! Deliver us through Your mercy, Your grace, Your uncompromising love, and Your unyielding power! Deliver us! In Jesus Name
My flesh and my heart may fail, but God is the strength of my heart and my portion forever. - Psalm 73:26

Good Morning Lord,
We come first to say thank You for granting us another opportunity to call on Your Name. You have been better than good to us.
We look at devastation in our world and hear those suffering saying I still have God.
What power those two words carry. But God.
We should've been dead and gone, But God.
We could have lost our minds by now, But God.
We lost our desire to go on, But God.
Grief overtook my soul, But God.
I don't know who can help me, But God.
We were headed down a one way street named self-gratification, headed for heartache and headaches, But God.
We tried to go back and pick up a failed relationship we had , But God.
The rumor others repeated was stopped before it became damaging, But God.
We never could have made it, But God.
We thought we could handle everything our way, But God stepped in and fixed up our mess.
Thank You Lord, for our But God moments. Before our But God moments we struggled with despair, disbelief, and darkness. After our But God intervention we had nothing but, Your light, Your love, and a new life. Thank You for our But God experiences where You provided relief and

redemption through Your marvelous mercy and generous grace.
Thank You Lord for granting us our But God encounter, for we know, we are where we are and who we are because of You!
In Jesus Name

Chapter 3 Love is an Action Word- Prayers of Love

"Love is patient, love is kind. It does not envy, it does not boast, it is not proud. It does not dishonor others, it is not self-seeking, it is not easily angered, and it keeps no record of wrongs."- 1 Corinthians 13:4-5

As a child I thought love was having my parents shower me with gifts, get me my favorite butter pecan ice cream cone or let me ride my bike until dusk. When I became a teenager, I thought love was the way a boy would follow me with his eyes down the hallway at school or try to sit by me on the bus and sneak a kiss. When I became a wife and mother, I started to understand the true meaning of love…. sacrifice, putting yourself last and making sure everyone else is taken care of and satisfied.

Isn't that what God did for us. He sacrificed His only son; let Him die so we could live. He stepped in and died to save all of us from death and destruction. That is love in action and yes that is love!!

For God so loved the world that he gave his only begotten Son that whoever believes in him should not perish, but shall have everlasting life-John 3:16

Dear Lord,
Thank you for this morning! We are so blessed to be able to see this day. Lord, You already know it's been a very long week. Thank You for ushering us into this new dawning.

Today we come to say thank You for Your great example of love and showing us what it means to love unconditionally. If we ever needed You and love this is the time, and this is the season.
Lord, prick our hearts so we can learn how to love without judgement and conditions! How to sense a person's heart and not their situation.

Give us insight so we can peel back the attitudes and behaviors we might not like and deal with the persons frailties to show them the love of Christ. Give us the courage not only to love on purpose, but with a purpose. Lord strengthen us so we will be bold enough to love our enemies, embrace our haters and love those who may never hear a kind word. Help us to remember love is sacrifice but it pays off in dividends.

Help us to show kindness to each other even those we don't know. Give us the energy we need to sow seeds of love and respect where other are sowing hate and disrespect. Lord guide us into the areas where love is being stomped out and let us be bold in our delivery and our exhibits of sowing seeds of

kindness and love!
Love never fails, it's not puffed up or boastful and love conquers all! Today we ask for our hearts to be filled with the love of Christ so we can start an unstoppable movement across this divided and hate filled world! A movement of loving each other out loud, on purpose and with an unending desire to love everyone as You have given us the ultimate example.
In Jesus Name,
Amen

**Above all, love each other deeply, because love covers a multitude of sins...
1 Peter 4:8**

Dear Lord,

Lord, today we come to say how much we love You. Your love for us is unlimited and knows no boundaries. We want to take a few minutes to express our love for You. In reality our vocabulary isn't extensive enough to convey the love, respect and gratitude we have for You.

When we stop and think about how you died for us, how you forgive us over and over again and how You never forsake us, we can't help but be grateful! Love is an action word and You have shown us countless times just how much You love us.
You supply our needs- action
You heal us- action
You keep us safe- action
You answer our prayers- action

Lord, we love You with our whole heart, we love You with every breathe we take, we love you when the sun comes up and when the sun sets. We love You during our good days and we love You during our challenging times. Lord, we love You because You loved us enough to create us in Your image. We love You, because You are a constant source of strength and You never leave us during our valley experiences.

Oh how we love You Lord, oh how we love You. We could go on and on and still never be able to truly

convey our love for You. Oh, how we love You, Lord. It's Sunday morning and we are so excited to be able to go to worship and give You the honor and all the glory that the Lord of Lord deserves.
Oh, how we love You, Lord. Thank You for Your example of love. Thank You for loving us! In Jesus Name, Amen

Be completely humble and gentle; be patient, bearing with one another in love. -
1 Corinthians 16:14

Dear Lord,
It's me again and I can't sleep, too much on my mind, so here I am coming to You to sort things out.

Today, I come asking that You fill me back up! Lord I am operating on fumes and I need my tank to be filled. These past few days have been trying and testing on so many different levels. I have been operating on the fumes of Your love, Your mercy, and Your grace.

Today, I come as humbly as I can asking that you fill me up Lord. I am sure there may be others who need to be replenished and right now I come on our behalf Lord asking for Your help. We need to be refilled with patience so we can listen quietly to those who share their pain and hurt with us. Let us be still enough to hear, see and feel what they are trying to convey. Then Lord, give us the right words to speak to them and for them as we pray for their situation to get better.

Please refresh our discernment so we will be able to identify those we need to walk away from or walk around. Lord, we have been depleted of our understanding and tolerance. Help us so we can understand those who would do evil against any of Your children and help us to be tolerant of those who are different.

Fill us up Lord, so we can continue to lift Your name and edify You! Please keep giving me the words I need to talk to You about all things whether great or small. Dear Lord, please fill us with Your Spirit so all we say, think or do is of You and not about ourselves!

I come asking that You refuel us with compassion and concern, so when one of our Christian sisters or brothers stumble or fall we can be there and provide a hand to pull them up, a knee to bend with them in prayer, a shoulder to lay on, a tear to shed with them and word from You to lift their spirit.

Thank You for refueling us, as only You can. Thank You for lifting our spirits, recharging our souls, reviving our desire to live a godly life, and filling us up with unspeakable joy, perfect peace, and unwavering love for You, ourselves, and others. Fill us up Lord, thank You for keeping us running this race with victory in our view!

I love You Lord.
Amen

Do everything in love. -1Corinthians16:14

Dear Lord,
There's joy in knowing Jesus loves me. Thank You Lord for this new day, this new opportunity, and this new chance.

I am so glad we serve a God who can turn our situation(s) around and work things out in our favor. It's amazing how God has already mapped out our journey and given us the tools we need to travel on our journey. All we need to do is trust, obey and move forward.

When we try to take charge of our lives without consulting God, without seeking confirmation and clarity, that's when we find ourselves lost in a self-imposed "bad situation". Lord, thank You for being a God of second chances and a God who can step in and turn our situation from bad to better.

As we navigate our way through our daily lives we make mistakes along the way. We are so grateful for Your grace and Your mercy which keeps blessing us, in spite of. Father, we realize we still will face consequences for our behavior, but You have already forgiven us. Thank You Lord!

Lord, help us so we won't be so hard headed, so bull headed and have our heads so high up in the clouds that we lose sight of the assignment that was given by You. Please continue to direct us down the path, which is righteous, responsible, and realistic. Guide our feet so we will walk in humility and honor. Purge our minds of all selfish and self-centered thoughts. Lord, open our eyes so we can stay clearly focused on our goals while reaching the finished line to hear You say, "well done".

Thank You for turning around that situation we were in which led to abusive behavior, thank You for rescuing us. Thank You for loving us like you do! Thank You, God, for turning around the situation with our family member, so they didn't lose a limb to diabetes or cancer.
Lord, we thank You, for turning around our financial situation, so we are no longer hiding from creditors calls. Thank You or loving us, love in action every time You step in. Oh, yes we thank You for turning around our situation with our spouse or significant other, allowing us now to be engaged in a healthy and happier relationship.

We love You so much Lord and we love serving a God of second chances. Thank You for being a God who can and who will, turn our situation around so everything is good and keeps getting better.

Thank You Lord! Thank You Lord!
In Jesus Name,
Amen

REFLECTION

Did your ability to love others change once you

started your faith walk? How?

____

____

____

What did you have to "let go of" to really fall in love

with yourself?

____

____

____

____

How do you show love towards those who are not always lovable?

____

____

____

____

____

____

Chapter 4 Faith over Fear- Prayers for Anxiety

BURYING WORRY AND FEAR- PRAYERS FOR ANXIETY

"So do not fear, for I am with you: do not be dismayed, for I am your God. I will strengthen you and help you: I will uphold you with my righteous right hand."

- Isaiah 41:10 NIV

In today's world we are all faced with dark days, days where we are worrying more than we are relaxing and days where we have such high anxiety, we make ourselves physically ill. Fear is real, depression is real, and anxiety can take over your whole life. Doctors can prescribe pills, therapy, and positive self-talk exercises. For some these things do work. I was in therapy, on anti-depressants, used wine to numb my pain and joined several self-help groups.
I got better when I let go of the guilt others had put on me. I really felt happy and all the weights lifted when I stopped living for others and started living for Him. This is why, I would like to recommend Jesus. You can have a one on one talk with Him; there is no judgement, no criticizing, and no pretentiousness. Jesus is always available, and he never tells you your time is up. Yes, I have found that He is the best medicine I could ever recommend – try Him, it is free.

Yea though I walk through the valley of the shadows of death, I will fear no evil for Thou areth with me-Psalm 23:4

Dear Lord,
Thank You for today. Thank You letting us make it through yesterday. We love You Lord.
Lord, You have brought us through many valley experiences, through dangers seen and unseen and yes, You have brought us through mess we created ourselves. The beauty in all of this is the word" through". Even in our moments of despair and distress while going through we weren't left stuck or abandoned in the situation.

While we were "going through", some of us were able to find strengths we never knew we had. The strength to hold on to our faith when darkness was all around us, the strength to speak Your Name when no other name could help and the courage to keep passing through our go through even as new road blocks, obstacles and challenges came our way.

Through....while going through we had to hold on to things which we could have lost and that would have made our situation unbearable. Things like the hymn we learned as a child, which we could hum while going through, Amazing Grace, Blessed Assurance and Oh How I Love Jesus. Lord, thank You for letting us be able to hold on to Your unchanging and unchangeable hand while we were in our go through period. Your hand steadied us, it stayed us, and it saved us from falling into our valley versus passing through it.

Thank You, for reminding us to hold onto Your Word while we were going through. Yea though we walk through the valley of the shadow of death, we shall fear no evil! Your words give us comfort and help us hold on.
Thanking You for the nails that went through Jesus hands and the spikes that went through His feet, so He couldn't come down from the cross. He died so we could live and through His death we received eternal life.
Thank You for Loving us through our sinful periods and through our disobedience. We say thank You because now we realize we must go through to have completion of our journey.

Through You we have life and have it in such an abundant manner.
Through You we gain access to the kingdom.
Through You we are blessed beyond measure.
Thanking You for our go through experiences and praising You for allowing through to be a process in which we never get STUCK.

In Jesus Name, **Amen**

**The Lord himself goes before you and will be with you; he will never leave you nor forsake you. Do not be afraid; do not be discouraged.
Deuteronomy 31:8**

*Dear Lord,
Thank You for a good night's rest and an early morning wake-up! Once again, we are blessed to see a new day!*

There are many who are struggling with depression, loneliness, and isolation during this time. Today we come Lord, asking that You will touch their minds and give them clarity. Lord, help them to be able to sort through their thoughts and find some sense of peace and security. Let them be reminded that You are their Heavenly Father and You are always with them.

Adjust their attitudes so they can choose laughter over lamenting, hope over helplessness, self-love over self-loathing and determination over depression. Lord, open their ears so they can hear Your word which can and will sustain them. Let them find comfort in knowing You are a mind regulator, heart fixer and an attitude adjuster.

Lord, give the loved ones, family and friends of those struggling with depression the right words to speak and the insight to know when to simply be still and let God handle the situation.

We come asking that You will blow a fresh wind of peace over their lives so chaos can be limited, blow a fresh wind of emotional strength over them so they will not succumb to depression. Lord, spark a fire in their soul and let it burn with encouragement and enlightenment.

Thank You for being a healer of our mind, a filter for our emotions and a keeper of our spirit. We love You Lord for lifting us from dark places and for elevating our attitudes to a new and intensified level in You. Thank You for the emotional breakthroughs, healings, and spiritual restorations You are about to manifest in us!!

In Jesus Name, Amen

I want to be free from anxieties- 1 Corinthians 7:32

Dear Lord,
Today we come asking that you will step in and help relieve those of us struggling with anxiety. Lord, sometimes in the busyness of life we forget that You are in control of every aspect of our life. We sit and worry about our finances, our families, our health, and we even worry about tomorrow while trying to make it through today. Lord, help us to stand on Your promises in Your Word.

Forgive us for getting weak and not leaning to Your understanding. Lord, help us to always remember You know all our needs and wants and there is no reason for anxiety or worry as You will supply all we need as we show ourselves worthy. Lord, please replace our fear and anxiety with increased faith and more trust in Your Word, Your will, and Your way. Help us to keep You as the nucleus of our lives so anxiety and worry have no place to rest.

Thank You for caring about us, loving us, and keeping us! Lord, we won't worry about tomorrow we will just live from day to day, because we know You hold tomorrow, and we know You hold our hand!! In Jesus Name,
Amen

For our light affliction, which is but for a moment, is working for us a far more exceeding and eternal weight of glory. -2 Corinthians 4:17

Lord,

Where people are feeling hopeless and lonely, we are asking that You will breathe winds of comfort and peace into their lives. For those who feel abandoned we ask that You provide protection and a safety net for them.

Lord, we need Your touch in so many different ways but today we come on behalf of the lonely, the abandoned and those with no hope.

Please touch their minds so the thoughts of giving in and giving up can be overcome with thoughts of "with Christ all things are possible". Help those of us who know You to live a life where we reach out and help those in despair. Where we obey Your commandment and love each other as You love us.

Lord, please protect, preserve, and provide for the least of them and for those who are   feeling in despair.
Thanking You in advance for Your loving kindness.
In Jesus name,
Amen

Trust in the Lord with all thine heart; and lean not unto thine own understanding. Prov 3:5

Lord,

Time seems to be moving so quickly. We are just in awe of this year, there's been tragedy, death, illness and so many challenges, yet we are still standing. Thank You Lord for keeping us through the various situations and for giving us the strength we needed to remain standing.

Today, we come asking for a boost in our emotional and mental wellbeing. Help us so we won't sink into any dark or unknown places in our minds and our thoughts. Life can become so daunting at times and we even question Why??? Lord, please give us emotional strength so we will lean not on our understanding, but truly trust and depend on you. Lord, please breathe peace and contentment over our souls so our minds will rest easy and we can continue to forge forward in Your will and Your way. We are taking one day at a time, knowing You are leading and guiding us along the way. We love You Lord; we praise You and we thank You for all You have done and are yet to do. In Jesus Name, Amen

Be steadfast, unmovable, always abounding in the work of the Lord.
1 Corinthians 15:58

Dear Lord,

It's me coming to you on this morning! I am so blessed to be able to have a secure place to lay my head. Thank You Lord.

We are living in times where the truth has become nonexistent, where bitterness, rancor and discord are the norm and where hatred reigns supreme. Lord, forgive us for not standing up, speaking up and changing up the divisive and ungodly atmosphere in our land. Lord, forgive us for being coward soldiers. Today, we come asking forgiveness for not being bold enough in our faith walk and our example to this world of what Christians act like and look like. Lord, we realize if we were to walk boldly, proclaim Your word louder and love others as You have loved us this world would be a better place.

Lord, You know our hearts and often times we make bad or unwise decisions which adversely impact others! Please forgive us for not being strong enough to stand up against those who violate Your word and Your will. Help us so we can be fully suited in the whole armor of God so we can fight against the darkness of this land. Yes,

Lord fortify our faith, increase our initiative, and expand our energy levels so we can fully wage war against the evil and corruption in this present age. Equip us with the "belt" of truth, the "breastplate" of righteousness, the "shield" of faith, the "helmet" of salvation, the "sword" of the spirit and cover our feet with peace as we walk. Let our tongues be used to speak truth to power by speaking Your word into others' lives. Let our hearts radiate with brotherly love and understanding.

More importantly Lord, now that we have sought forgiveness for not being strong soldiers we come asking that You walk with us as we become bolder in our witness, unashamed in our faith walk and as we stand firm and fast against the evils of this land. Lord, thank You for renewing our resolve to be steadfast in our Christian walk and to live a life which is pleasing in Your sight. Thank You for forgiving us for our short comings and thank You for another opportunity   to get things together.
In Jesus Name,
Amen

Trust in the Lord and do good; dwell in the land and enjoy safe pasture. -

Psalm 37:3

Dear Lord,
Here I am again. Today I come simply to say thank You for keeping me and covering me. Thank You for not turning away from me.

Sometimes we have to be reminded that trusting You is so much more rewarding than trusting man. Today we come with our hands lifted high ready to receive whatever blessings you have for us. We come realizing that our needs are more important than our wants and we are thanking You right now Lord for fulfilling our needs!! You continue to show us who is in control, yet we tend to get ahead of ourselves at times thinking we have everything all together on our own.

Lord, thank You for the reminders that You have in place to keep us humble and focused on You being in control. Alarm clocks because only You can wake us up suddenly without assistance, so we won't be late. Breathing in and out as only You could blow breath into our bodies so we could freely exhale and inhale. Yes, and even having the correct words come out of our mouths because You formed our brain to work in conjunction with our mouth. Thank You for being the reason that we exist.

Today, we acknowledge that you are Lord all by yourself, without any assistance from us. We ask that You forgive us when we have slipped up and put our trust in man and worldly things. We come today Lord, realizing that all of our trust needs to be in You, as You are a God who knows no failure and never fails Your children.

Thanking You in advance for guaranteeing our needs, supplying our wants and always being our on time Savior! Trusting You Lord even when I can't trace or touch YOU. Trusting You Lord because You are truly all we really need.
In Jesus Name
Amen

REFLECTION

Do you ever feel like it's just too much and you are so tired? If you could remove weights from your life what would they be?

____

____

____

____

Make a list of five things that you worry about. Then make a list of what you would ask God to do to handle it.

____

____

____

____

____

____

____

____

____

Chapter 5: Prayers for Our Families

Fathers, do not exasperate your children; instead, bring them up in the training and instruction of the Lord- Ephesians 6:4

The family structure has been under assault for years. Fathers are absent, mothers are overwhelmed, children are often left to be in charge of everything and so it goes. The family unit has been stretched, strained and in many cases just plain old dysfunctional.
What looks like family to one may not look like family to another. Families are different, their makeup, their moral code, their structure, and their faith foundations.

I am blessed that I grew up in a two-parent home and I had three younger siblings. We knew our grandparents, our aunts, uncles, and cousins by the busload. We had Walker family gatherings on Thanksgiving, Ballew family time in the summer and lots of visits in between. Family, the second greatest gift God granted us after the sacrificial love of His only Son.

As I grew older and started my own family it took on a different meaning to have my own children, my own home and own household. I really learned what it meant to lean and depend on Jesus when my youngest daughter was born prematurely and almost died at the age of 9 months from a severe case of pneumonia and asthma. When the doctors told her father and I to call our family because it was bad, I went to a corner of the hospital and simply prayed. I asked God to spare her, take me if you need someone now and please give me an opportunity to raise my child. She is 33 years old as I pen type this page. Look at God.

Family over everything is a very nice catch phrase, but in fact God created the family unit so we could be together and take care of one another.

Believe in the Lord Jesus, and you will be saved-you and your household, Acts 16:31

Dear Lord,
Thank you for this day. There is just something about an early morning rising and conversation with You that keeps my heart happy and my soul satisfied.

Lord, today we come to say thank You for the firm foundation we have been given. Thank You Lord, for our praying mothers, Bible believing fathers, Christ centered grandparents and our spiritual community of extended family and friends. A tree is known by the fruit it bears. Just like a tree we are recognized by the fruits we bear. So many families are struggling with generational curses as their fruit lies dormant or falls rotten to the ground. They were not planted into a fertile and solid foundation of prayer, faith, the scriptures, study of the Word and application of it in our daily lives, which is so unfortunate.

We come to say thank You for the roots of our tree being so deep in its foundation. Deep enough to be saturation by the many showers of blessings You grant us daily. Our roots are deep enough not to get tangled up with the chaos and mess of trees which are only covered by surface dirt and not covered by divine grace! Yes, we say thank You for the nutrients in our soil which caused our roots to be strong and durable. Those nutrients of powerful prayers, passionate praise, and amazing grace.

Lord, just like the deeply planted tree we want to be unmovable and unshakable in our faith walk and our spiritual life. We say thank You for the good fruits we are bearing, which help us edify You and give You the highest praise. Fruits of service, kindness, patience, sharing, sacrificing, spreading love and so much more. The fruits of gratitude and gratefulness; that cause us to thank You Lord for being a real presence in our lives.

Thank You for our foundation, thank You for deep and developed roots. We want to be mindful at all times of the fruits we bear, and we always want to use our fruits for Your glory and to show You honor. We say Glory to God for our deeply entrenched roots which keep us locked into our solid foundation-Jesus Christ.

In the precious name of Jesus,

Amen.

Honor your father and mother, so that you may live long in the land the Lord your God is giving you- Exodus 20:12

Good Morning Lord,
Today, we come asking for restoration of family structure, family values and family unity. We are asking for a renewed spirit to rise up in parents, single parents, young parents, stepparents, and grandparents. Our children have lost their way and we can't keep blaming it on society and drugs. It's time for parents to reclaim their role and restore values, morals, and decency back to the family.

Lord, help us to get back to parents modeling respect, integrity, and truth for their children versus reckless behavior, indecent lifestyles and taunting one another. Give parents the foresight and strength they need to put down the guns and their video games and pick up their Bibles and talk to their children. Help them to see that material things are no substitute for nurturing and caring for their children. Open their hearts so they can feel the emptiness their children are feeling due to disconnected relationships. Touch their minds so they can reach back in their memories and pull up the home training they received will sitting on grandma's lap or while holding their mother's hands.

Lord, give parents the will power they need to stop

being their child's friend and return to be the parent. Renew the parent's spirit so they won't be weary while providing a safe haven for their children. Give the parents a burning desire to return to the basics, eating dinner together, turning the electronic devices off and having open and honest conversations with their children about life and about you. Restore a sense of self-worth in the parents, revive their spiritual side and renew their mindset so they can be energized to make family unity and togetherness a positive priority.

Lord, fill them with love that is coupled with discipline and appropriate reactions to their children's behavior. Give them wisdom to use their parenting skills in a loving-yet instructive way. Lord, let there be a tidal wave of positive self-esteem, proactive self-awareness, and prudent self-discipline in homes across this land. Let prayer replace arguing, let love overcome anger, let honest communication eliminate dishonesty and let family values replace family erosion.

In the matchless name of Jesus,

Amen

Carry each other's burdens, and in this way, you will fulfill the law of Christ- Galatians 6:2

Dear Lord,
Today we come first to say thank You for keeping Your hand of protection over us through the night. Thank You, for waking us up this morning to see a new day!

Father, You are the giver of all life, creator of all things and the fixer of everything which is broken. As the master of all miracles You hold the entire world in Your hands.
Lord, today we come asking for strength for those who are serving as caregivers for their loved ones who are dealing with terminal illnesses or end of life diseases. Please provide a sense of peace for these faithful and loving souls, who often put their lives on pause to be available for their loved ones.

Lord, we come asking for strength for the caregivers to realize that they are not alone in this journey. We are asking for Your divine touch to give caregivers permission to release and let go of their feelings of fear, grief, and sorrow. Build them up on every leaning side so they might feel Your love and use it as fuel to continue to provide for their loved one. Instill in the caregiver the will power they need to not only exercise their faith but practice Your promise of never leaving or forsaking us through their fervent prayers for the patient they are tending to.

Lastly Lord, we are asking for Your anointed covering over the caregivers so they can exhibit signs of hope, faith, and trust in Your will for whatever the outcome might be. Thank you for these loving, patient and caring souls who dedicate their time, energy, and love to providing a positive and loving atmosphere for their loved ones and those under their care as they deal with their terminal illnesses.

Help all who are involved to remember God is in control and He never fails.
In Jesus Name,
Amen

REFLECTION

What is your definition of family? How has your family structure shaped the person you are today?

____

____

____

____

____

____

____

____

____

____

____

____

Is there a breakdown in the family's role in society in the 21st century? How can we change that?

____

____

____

____

____

____

____

____

____

Chapter 6 Lord, Deliver Me- Prayers of Deliverance and Spiritual Growth

"I lift up my eyes to the hills, from whence cometh my help. My help cometh from the Lord, which made heaven and earth."-Psalm 121:1-2 KJV

Life is filled with swift transitions, many ups and downs and indeed its filled with a lot of decision making. Once we decide to follow Christ, turn our lives over to Him we must truly trust the process. The process, which includes staying focused on what lies ahead and letting go of what used to be.

Lord, I have need deliverance for so many things, bitterness, hurt, mistreatment, low self-esteem, the list goes on. Some need deliverance from drugs, alcohol, a lying tongue and much more. When we struggle to the point where the person, we are hurting the most is ourselves we truly need deliverance.

Deliverance can only be obtained when we truly learn how to relinquish and let God handle the situation. Only God can fix us, heal us, and yes deliver us. Sometimes we must hit the bottom to rise with full power and full awareness of who we are, who delivered us and how grateful we should be. Lord, please deliver us from ourselves.

The steps of a good man are ordered by the Lord: and he delighteth in his way. -Psalm 37:23

Dear Lord,

Lord, I want to come humbly today to ask that You order my steps through this journey called life. Lord, I want to live a life that not only pleases You, but one that honors You. Help me so I can always be mindful of my actions, so I won't offend, oppress, or ostracize anyone. Lord, order my steps so I can be a light in dark places, leading others to You. Let me be a voice of reason in the midst of chaos and an example of love where there is animosity. Lead me and guide me as I walk through this journey called life. Please order all my steps Lord! Lord, please order my steps so wherever I walk it will leave footprints of truth, loyalty, obedience, and forgiveness. Yes, please order my steps so I will follow You, be guided by You and walk closer to You.

In Jesus Name, Amen

Brothers and sisters, if someone is caught in sin, you who live by the Spirit should restore that person gently. But watch yourselves, or you also may be tempted. -Galatians 6:1

Dear Lord,
I come today with a simple request. Sometimes we get so caught up on other people's flaws we fail to see our own shortcomings and flaws. Lord, today I am asking that You fix me! Lord fix my tongue, so I won't use it in any evil or hurtful way and hold my hands Lord, so I won't use them in a way which dishonors service to You! Lord, guide my steps and light my path so I won't get caught in someone else's lane or disrupt someone's path to You. Fix my heart Lord so I can love the unlovable, have compassion for the untouchable and reach out to the unreachable. Please fix my mind so it will be filled with thoughts of love, worship, thanksgiving, peace and service, not depressed and unhealthy thoughts. Yes, today I am stopping by Lord in need of a tune up from You! Fix me Lord so my light will shine bright, Your love will shine through and my walk will be a living testimony. Fix me Jesus fix me!

In Jesus Name,
Amen

And I am sure of this, that he who began a good work in you will bring it to completion at the day of Jesus Christ- Philippians 1:6

Dear Lord,

Once again, I am here to see a new dawning! Thank You for Your unmerited favor. Lord, today I want to pray for increased strength so I can be a strong branch connected to the True Vine (You). Help me so I will bear good fruit and not have any brittle or withered branches growing from me. Yes, Lord I am asking to be rejuvenated and recharged so I can be a strong and fruit bearing branch. I ask that my works speak for me and not a boastful or arrogant attitude. I ask that You allow me to bear fruit that is in line with the fruits of the spirit, love, peace, joy, patience, understanding, goodness, kindness, self-control, and faithfulness. In this year of elevation Lord, I come asking for elevated strength to make sure I am a working, serving, loving, and willing branch of the True Vine or Tree of Life, which is You! Thank You for my connection which keeps me nourished and strong in my walk with you!

Amen and Amen!

And pray that we may be delivered from wicked and evil people, for not everyone has faith. -2 Thessalonians 3:2

Dear Father God,

Thank you, Lord! Right now, I am coming asking that You will keep me connected to the right power source. Lord, lead me and guide me so I don't stray and become caught up in things of the world, which are harmful and no good. As we have corruption in the highest levels of government, truth is now an obsolete thing. Lies rule and human decency is an extinct commodity.

Lord please keep me plugged into You as my source of light, energy, and my overall power source. As long as I can stay connected to You through my prayers, my study, and my worship I won't fall prey to the wickedness of this world. Lord help me so I can show others there is a choice to be made. They can plug into Your power source which emits love, truth, peace and understanding. Versus the dark and deadly power source which emits division, deceit, lies and hatred. Thank you for being my power source Lord. One that never dies out, corrodes, or becomes unusable.

In Jesus name; the Power of all Powers,

Amen.

Know this, my beloved brothers: let every person be quick to hear, slow to speak and slow to anger- James 1:19

Here I am Lord,

Thankful for another night You kept me and another morning You have allowed me to see. Today I come asking that You will elevate my hearing into listening. Help me so I can truly listen to those who come to me in distress or just in need of an ear to pour their concerns or sorrows into. Help me Lord so I won't judge, so I won't turn off and so I won't rebuke whoever it is that needs a true listening ear. Lord, I realize listening requires discernment, patience, and compassion, please help me to be able to show compassion while discerning the real message through patiently and actively listening to whomever needs my listening ear. Thank You for elevating my levels of hearing into levels of compassionate listening. As today I pray Lord, I also ask that You continue to speak to my heart. I am listening God and I am being obedient to Your desire and call over my life. Thank you and please help me to always be a listener and not just a hearer.

In Jesus name,

Amen.

Bearing with one another and if one has a complaint against another, forgiving each other, as the Lord has forgiven you so you also must forgive Matthew 6:12

Lord,

Today I come asking for forgiveness of all our sins. I am asking for wisdom and common sense to do the right things and not stray. Lord, You made it very plain with the ten commandments. I come asking for truth to always be in my mouth and on my tongue; I am asking for love to win out over hate so that the killing may stop. I come asking for all jealous spirits to become spirits of unity where we lift one another. Lord, help me to do the right thing especially when the wrong thing is so much more enticing and inviting. Help me to embrace, honor and live the ten commandments which You gave us centuries ago. Lastly Lord, I am asking that you fix my heart, fix my mouth so all I do is to honor and uplift you as I do the right things.

In Jesus name,

Amen.

To whom much is given, much will be required- Luke 12:48

Lord,

In your Word it says to whom much is given, much is required. Lord, today I come asking for guidance so I can do all that is required of me. Open my eyes so I can see the direction in which You are ordering my steps. Unplug my ears so I can hear Your voice and not get confused with my desires. I want to clearly hear Your will for me Lord. Give me a caring heart and willing hands so I can serve those who are helpless; lift up those who are down; listen to those who have no one to talk to and sit with someone who is lonely. Lord, You have blessed me with many riches, such as, family, love, peace of mind, and unspeakable joy. Help me now so I can be a tree that bears good fruit. Lord I want to be able to share my fruits of love, joy, peace, patience, kindness, faithfulness, gentleness, goodness, and self-control with others. Yes, to whom much is given, much is required. Lord, I am available to You to be used in your service and be a true servant. Thank you for choosing me and thank you for helping me to understand that it's better to be a laborer that bears good fruits than a weed that strangles out the vine.

I love you Lord,

Amen.

He does not deal with us according to our sins, nor repay us according to our iniquities. For as high as the heavens are above the earth, so great is his steadfast love towards those who fear him. Psalm10-11

Good Morning Father,
Thank You for this morning. Lord, I am so grateful to be able to offer up this my feeble prayer.

Today, we come asking for forgiveness of all our sins. It's not an easy road, there are curves, hills, and valleys along the way. Often, we step outside of the will and commands of our Lord. Please forgive us when we stray. Give us increased awareness and stronger will power so we can stay with the confines of Gods will and His way. We are asking for wisdom and common sense to do the right things and not stray. Lord, You made it very plain for us with the 10 commandments.

We come asking for truth to always be in our mouth and on our tongues, we are asking for love to win out over hate so all these killings may stop; and we come asking for all jealous spirits to become spirits of unity and lifting up one another. Lord, help us as individuals to do the right thing especially when the wrong thing is so much more enticing and inviting.

Help us to embrace, honor and live within the 10 commandments and abide by Your laws as well as mans' law. Lastly Lord, I am asking that you would fix our hearts, give us clean hearts, and fix our minds to be stayed on You. Please fix our mouths so all we say

*is to reverence and uplift Your Holy Name. Yes, Lord
please forgive us of all our sins, while helping us live
our lives within the boundaries of Your laws while
abiding by mans' law.*
In Jesus Name,
Amen

"May the favor of the Lord our God rest on us; establish the work of our hands for us- yes establish the work of our hands." Psalm 90;17–

Dear Lord,
Thank you for bringing us to this morning. We are so blessed to be counted in the number of those who are still here!

As we move forward in this journey called life, it is very important for us to always remember! Lord, when we look into the rear-view mirror of our lives, we see so many things! Things we want to forget, things we want to bury and things we want no one else to ever know!

Right now we come saying thank You for the things we are seeing in our rear-view mirror. Thank You for the valleys You walked through with us, never leaving us to get stuck in our valley experience! Lord we thank You for the disappointment and dysfunction You carried us through never allowing us to become distanced from You.

We thank You for the pain that You turned into purpose, the worry You turned into worship, the grief You covered with grace and the hurt You removed with healing!

Lord, we don't want to keep looking over our shoulder and looking in our rear view mirror, but we do want to remember where we have been and how we made it! Thank You Lord for rearview reminders that always help us know that You are always in control!

Thank You for grace and mercy that have no boundaries and no limits! Thank You for allowing us to be able to look back and truly see how far You have brought us not from but out of! Out of brokenness, out of bondage, out of loneliness, out of depression and out of desperation! Thank You for our forward view! Thank You for preparing us for our season of flying high and our season of overcoming! Thank You Lord for all things past and all things present!
In Jesus Name,
Amen

You are my hiding place; you will protect me form trouble and surround me with songs of deliverance-Psalm 32:7

Lord,

Here we are once again saying thank You for allowing us to still be here! Thank You Lord. As we get so hurried keeping up with the instant pace of our daily routines, we often take a short cut or an easy way out. Sometimes while doing this we slip back into our worldly ways. This causes our old habits to rise up and we fall prey to mess and messiness, sin!!

Today, we come asking you to rescue us from ourselves and from sliding backwards. Lord, the little lie we told to make ourselves look more important than we are, the whispering we did to someone about our friends business and ignoring that stranger who needed help simply because they looked different than us, Lord, please rescue us from ourselves! Lord rescue us from using alcohol as a sedative to numb our pain and from using illegal drugs to help us escape our difficult situation. Please save us from our over thinking which often leads us to a dark and lonely place, please Lord rescue us!

Rescue us from our egos and from our arrogance when we think we are bigger and more relevant than we really are. Save us from our ignorance when we think we know everything, but in reality, we do not know much at all! Yes, Lord rescue us from ourselves. Fill our hearts with Your true agape love, penetrate our minds so we will have pure thoughts and keep Your commandments. Guide our hands so we will use them to uplift and serve, not point, and tear down, rescue us from ourselves!!

Lord thank You for allowing grace and mercy to be our companions, because if You poured out justice on us, we would be paying for so many of our sins, but You sparred us again. We come asking forgiveness for all our sins and thanking You in advance for Your gracious gifts of mercy, grace, and love. Thank You for rescuing us from falling prey to ourselves! Thank You for salvation that is free and available to us all. Lord, rescue us from ourselves and restore us back to a place where we are walking in Your will, living in Your favor and being the best people that we can be! Rescue us from ourselves, in Jesus' name, Amen.

Do not be conformed to this world, but be transformed by the renewal of your mind, that by testing you may discern what is the will of God, what is good and acceptable and perfect. - Romans 12:2

Dear Lord,

Lord, sometimes it seems as if we are not giving You our best. We hold back on our worship, our praise, our prayers, our love for one another and our works. Today, I am coming asking that you make us better.

Make us better examples of Your love, Your compassion, Your patience, and Your kindness. Help us to be examples of what better looks like. Lord, elevate our levels of communication so we are glorifying You in our speech. Please, help us to do better in our sharing the load. When we say we have left it at the altar, let us truly leave there. Better is our goal.

Please strengthen us so we can do better in reaching out and praying for one another, being there for each other and understanding how to really be a leaning post for others. Better. Lord, our goal is to be better in bringing light into dark places, hope where it has dwindled and help where it is needed. Better.

In Jesus Name,
Amen

Be still and know that I am God. I will be exalted among nations; I will be exalted in the earth. - Psalm 46:10

Good Morning Lord,
Lord I come today asking for peace in the midst of whatever storm someone might be in. We all know that once we get past the eye of the storm things get better. Help us to hold on!
Lord restore peace where there is confusion, renew hope where there is despair and replace fear with a faith and trust in knowing God is in control.
Help me(us) to get out of Your way and allow You to fix whatever is wrong. Lord help me(us) to relinquish the animosity and angst we might be holding in our hearts and let it be replaced with understanding and love. Lord, give us peace in the midst of drama and traumatic situations. Help us to remember all our help comes from You. Let us get out of our own way!! Thank ya!

Lord, please restore civility where there is discord, reignite the flames of respect instead of backbiting, reinstatement the bonds of friendship where trust has been broken and Lord please release peace and a peace of mind where confusion has been wreaking havoc.

Let us get reconnected to our power source and remain humble and kind in our dealings with each other. Lord, please hear our plea and allow things to be calm and peaceful no matter what the situation. Please Lord bring peace to all situations through Your power! Peace be still! Amen

"I can do all things through Him who gives me strength." Philippians 4:13

Dear Lord,
Thank you for today and for another opportunity to talk with You. Today I come saying thank you for the outcomes I have received during so many trials, test, and just everyday living. Lord, I pray for continued growth in how I carry myself, my character, my relationships, and my walk with You.   Please give me more discernment so I can weed out the toxic or needy people coming into my life; before I allow them to get in and affect my atmosphere. Give me patience so I can stand strong as I run this race called life. I do not want to give up or give in when things don't go as planned. Lord, give me understanding so I will forgive myself for past mistakes, letting go of poor decisions and releasing all jealousy and envy; focusing on what is mine, not someone else's. Lord help me to realize I may have started out on shaky ground but with and through You, I can accomplish all things. I thank you for never giving up on me and for Your amazing and unmatched love for me. Thank You for forgiveness, favor, and the ability to finish better than I started. Lord I am so grateful that it's not where I started, but where and how I finish. In Jesus name, Amen.

There is none like You, O Lord; You are great, and great is Your name in might. -Jeremiah 10:6

Good Morning Lord,
What an amazing morning it is and I am here to say Thank You Lord.

On this glorious morning, I am filled with joy all because I woke up realizing You know my name. Lord, I am not only referring to my birth name, but I am also making reference to my God given name, Your daughter, and Your child. What a blessing to know the Father knows all of His children.

Lord, You also know us by the name of Worrier, when our faith isn't as strong as it should be and we are trying to control only what You can. Forgive us for not leaving it in Your hands and walking by faith. We realize we must do better.

You know us by the name Disciple when we are walking in Your way and living in Your will. When we live by Your commandments and treat each other with Christian love, we know it pleases You. That is our hearts desire.

Lord, You know our name as Beloved when we are studying Your word, allowing Your spirit to reign in our lives and when people can see Your light in us. Yes, You know us by the name, Solider, when we are dedicated and committed to working in the vineyard, working to build up the Kingdom of God and spread the good news. You know us by Solider as we fight to defeat sin and we fight to protect all that You have given us. As we pray daily for strength, grace, mercy, forgiveness and as we intercede on others behalf, You know our name as Prayer Warrior. We are grateful that through our faith walk we have learned how to pray and what to pray for, whether it be prayers of comfort, thanksgiving, or specific request.

When we lift Your name up and show honor to You, You know us by the name, Worshipper. Not a day goes by when our hearts aren't touched by Your love and our minds blown by the way You bless us. This causes us to praise and worship You. Oh, it is such an awesome and indescribable feeling to know that You know our name, no matter which name it might be.

Oh, how marvelous and magnificent You are as, You know all, see all, created all and control all. We are so enormously grateful and abundantly blessed because You know our name. What's in a name, everything when that name is connected to the relationship and kinship we share with our Heavenly Father.

Your love is limitless, and Your blessings are too numerous to keep track of! I love you Lord and on today I come to say thank You for knowing my name and the names of all Your children.
In Your Precious Name,
Amen

For the Lord will not abandon His people on account of His great name, because the Lord has been pleased to make you a people for himself. - 1 Samuel 12:22

Lord,

Here we today asking for strength to let go, forgive, and move on! We have suffered hurt from family, friends, church members, coworkers and even strangers over the course of this year and during our journey called life.

Lord, please help us to leave baggage such as bitterness, anger, distrust and hurt behind us and not drag those negative forces with us. Give us the will power and strength to leave messy people behind. Lord, please help us to truly let go of the animosity and hurt so we can have inner peace and move forward not dwelling in a painful past.

Thanking You for the power of prayer which can help us to truly let go and let God! Thank You for releasing the anger and hurt off our shoulders as we forgive those who trespassed against us. Please Lord, give us the power to forgive and strength to move forward while embracing our future and letting go of our past.

In Jesus Name, Amen

Submit yourselves then to God, Resist the devil, and he will flee from you-James 4:7

Good Morning Lord,
Thank You for another restful night and an early morning wake up call.
Lord, I woke up this morning thinking of all the dead-end streets you saved me from. Thank You for steering me in a different direction when I thought I knew where I was going. Lord, You snatched me from the jaws of death and for that all I can say is thank You!
When I thought I had all the answers and I was in charge of my destiny you stepped in and provided a detour to what could have been my demise.
All the preparations and plan that I made without consulting You first could have ended in a bad way, but You rescued me by providing a detour to what otherwise could have been a dead end.
It's amazing how we map out what we think our lives should look like and how things should unfold without ever talking to You about anything. You allow grace and mercy to step in and provide a detour from the self-destructive path we were on.
Lord, I come today saying thank You for the detour You provided so I didn't stay on the avenue of self-indulgence and greed; thank You for steering me off of Lustful Lane and Backstabbers Boulevard.
I am so grateful that You provided a detour which kept me from going down Haters Highway and getting on Rebellious Rd. You kept me from going down Selfish Street and turning onto All About Me Avenue. Lord, I am so grateful for the detours You provided which saved me from myself!
I have learned how to call on You and ask for

*guidance, clarity, and direction. I realize now that
when You order my steps and direct my path life is so
much simpler and filled with blessings.*
*Thank You Lord for the detours and for being the
Light on my pathway, the Compass for my journey
and my Master way-maker.*
*I am grateful for the detours that saved me, changed
me and kept me.*
In the Mighty Name of Jesus,
Amen

REFLECTIONS

After you have identified what you need deliverance from sometimes it helps to make a "To Do List". What would yours look like?

____

____

____

____

____

____

____

____

____

What steps do you put in place no to fall prey to the same challenges again?

____

____

____

____

____

____

____

____

____

Chapter 7. God is in Control-Prayers for Pandemics and Turmoil

"If we confess our sins, He is faithful and just and will forgive us our sins and purify us from all unrighteousness.

-1st John 1:9

The United States has been so polarized and divided over the past few years. Hatred seems to be the flavor of the day every day and violence has become a badge of honor. Politics has become a sport and the dirtiest and most obnoxious person seems to always win. In my heart, I do believe that at our core America is not totally bad, just misguided and sometimes very unaware. I do know that God is in control and for that I very grateful.

In this season of political chaos, worldwide pandemics, and racial discord and just overall confusion, I am so comforted to truly believe that God has the whole world in His hands. He is the author and creator of all, and He knew our ending when He granted us or beginning. There truly is nothing out of His control and nothing that He cannot handle.

**For God is not a God of confusion but of peace.
1 Corinthians 14:33**

*Dear Heavenly Father,
Thank You for this day, Your loving protection, and
Your loving kindness. Lord, we love You with our
whole heart.*

*We come today seeking peace of mind, a settling of
our spirits and healing of a land that's filled with
chaos, untruths, and confusion. Today we are all
one click away from losing our sanity whether it's
over the coronavirus19, the failing stock market,
rampant gun violence in our inner cities or drug
abuse. Lord, we are coming right now asking for a
spiritual awaking, a divinely inspired intervention and
a powerful hedge of protection for all Your children.*

*We come today seeking Your guidance as this world
is dealing with a medical pandemic, COVID19,
sweeping from country to country, leaving behind
death, devastation and financial decay. Only You,
God can protect and heal our land. We are living in
such a precarious and perilous time. Youth shooting
each other down as a sport, parents abandoning
and killing their own children and world leaders
governing with their egos rather than an interest in
their constituents. Lord, heal our land.*

*As this medical plague rolls from one continent to
the next, let this be one a humbling experience for
those who think they can make it without You in their*

lives. Lord, please protect us from the deadly virus as well as the corruption and disintegration of a healthy and holy society. Let us try to find our way back to You, by turning from our sinful and wicked ways.

Help us to get back to a place-where we respect one another, work cooperatively with others and worship You in spirit and total truth. Lord, help us to stop using religion and our relationship with You as some type of qualifier for elite status in today's world. Lord please prick the hearts of those in leadership who are messing with people's livelihoods and let them get back to being led by Your laws, Your love and You leading us daily.

Lord, we need a touch from You to end this pandemic, stop all this gun violence and curb our sinful nature. Help us to turn from these wicked and hateful ways and restore accountability, respect, love, and decency back into our society. Lord, we know You hold the cure in Your hand, we know You can stop the violence with Your hands lifted high and yes, we know You are taking care of things as we pray and we are very grateful.

As I close my mind reflects back to numerous stories in Your word, the Bible, which describes mayhem, dysfunction and separation. Lord, we don't want to be separated from You, Your word, or Your way. Please Dear Lord, heal our land and restore us back *to a sacred sweet and nurturing relationship with You, especially in times of chaos and dysfunction. In Jesus Name, Amen*

God can bless you abundantly, so that in all things at all times, having all that you need, you will abound in every good work.

2 Corinthians 9:8

Dear Lord,
We thank You Lord for this new morning. Your new mercies and we are so grateful.
My heart has been filled with joy and my spirit is uplifted! Lord, because of You and our relationship I can smile in the midst of strange times. Lord, You have kept us free from hurt, harm and danger and for that we say thank You.

Lord, as we go about our day to day activities please keep us covered with Your mighty and majestic powers of protection and grant us a day filled with positive vibes and peaceful interactions. We are so thankful for the stillness we have had over these past few weeks. Being able to reflect and revive our spirits has been such a blessing.

Sometimes we get too busy to take time out to look at where we were and where we are. Today, we want to thank You for our right now blessings.
Right now, we aren't sick, thank You!
Right now, we aren't hungry, thank You!
Right now, we are not alone, even if we are physically isolated; we still have You and all Your glory!

Right now, we are not afraid, You are always with us.
Right now, we are loved like none other; Your love is uncompromised and unchanging.
Right now, we are grateful, for Your forgiveness toward us; Your mercies granted to us and Your love which envelopes us.
Yes thank You for our "Right Now".

In Your precious name, Amen

A man without self-control is like a city broken into and left without walls.
Proverbs 25:28

Dear Lord,

Thank You Lord for keeping us, even in the midst of all this chaos and confusion. We are living in this politically and racially divided atmosphere, where civility and truth are struggling to stay viable in this world of chaos. I say thank You for being the ultimate controller-being in control of all people, places, all situations, and all things.

Father, I stretch my hands to Thee, no other help I know. Lord please don't withdraw yourself from me. I truly will have nowhere to go!! We want to thank You for giving us one of the best gifts anyone could ever ask for or receive   the gift of

*eternal and everlasting life. Life, because
of Your miraculous birth, followed by Your
appointed death and Your transforming lifesaving
resurrection, we live.*

*Life, through the best and only real plan of
Salvation available!*
Life more abundantly because of You!
*Life with the family You designed and assigned us
to!*
*Life, a Christian journey where Your love, Your
forgiveness and Your unmerited grace and mercy
cover us.*
*Life, not always an easy road, but one we can
navigate with You ordering our steps.*
In Jesus Name,
Amen

You keep in in perfect peace whose mind is stayed on you, because he trusts in you. Isaiah 26:3

Dear Lord,

Daily we must make decisions, respond to challenges, and figure out which way to go. Sometimes it is decisions which are life and death decisions, family altering choices and complicated situations. Lord, it's not that our faith is wavering, or we trust You any less, it's just why me, why us and why now? Lord, help us to understand that it's not the why but The Who that counts. Help us to understand that sickness, tragedy or whatever the challenge didn't fall on us or our loved one because of who we are or what we did, but because of Who You Are in our lives. Help us Lord to understand trusting Your Will is always best, even when it's not easy. Watching our spouse slowly be stolen away by cancer, burying our children while we still live on or being diagnosed with a chronic illness which will change our lives forever is by no means easy.

Lord, help us to remember it is easier if we trust You, communicate our fears to You and let You walk us through the process. Lord, help us to lean and depend on You, keeping You as the center of our lives and the nucleus of our   relationships. Lord, thank You for being The Who, the Answer to our why's and our why nots. Lord, thank You for keeping us through every challenge and situation, so we can tell others and show them Who You are and what You can do. We are glad to realize that we need not worry about the why, but cling to the who. In Jesus Name, Amen

You God are all I have and all I need; my future is in Your hands-Psalm 16:5

Dear Heavenly Father,

We come today seeking healing of a land that's turned from You. We come asking for divine intervention on behalf of so many people who are being used as pawns by our government and political leaders. We come today seeking Your guidance because America has become too arrogant, too self-indulged and too worldly to realize that only God can heal our land. Lord, it is heartbreaking to look at all the blatant racism, hatred, and hypocrisy in America as people claim we are making America great again. Lord, please help us get back to a place-where we respected one another, worked cooperatively with others, and worshipped You not politicians. Lord please prick the hearts of those in leadership who are messing with people's livelihoods. Lord, we need a touch from You to heal our land. Help us to turn from these wicked and hateful ways and restore respect and decency back into our society. We need Thee Lord we need Thee right now!!
Amen

The Lord is my rock and my fortress and my deliverer, My God, my rock, in whom I take refuge, my shield and the horn of thy salvation, my stronghold. Psalm 18:2

Lord,

Here we are thanking You for one more day and for allowing our loved ones to still be here on this side. Thank You.

We marvel at Your almighty and omnipresent power! Your hand of protection and safety continues to keep us as we manage our way through this lingering pandemic. Lord, thank You for not only keeping our family safe, but all those families all over this land that You have cradled in Your arms of safety, protection, and provision.

Now this morning our prayer is simply to say Thank You for Keeping us all Safe In Your Arms! We are grateful that indeed You do have the whole world in Your hands! Your arms shield us from all the evils and traps set by our adversary. Your arms of contentment and calm cradle us and hold us when we are anxious. Your arms of love and compassion soothe our loneliness, depression, and feelings of being unwanted.

Lord thank You for your strong arms that reach down and pick us up when we have fallen, your steady arms which hold us when we feel weak. Lord, thank You for your benevolent arms which provide for us and carry blessings which You shower on us. Thank You Lord, for your loving, patient, and lifesaving arms. In Jesus name, Amen

He will wipe every tear from their eyes. There will be no more death or mourning, or crying or pain, for the old order of things has passed away. Revelations 21:4

Lord,
On today I come asking for a divine touch of healing over sickness and pain that's attacking someone's body at this time. Praying that Your will be done, while restoring their hurting and diseased body on today. Lord, give them the strength they need to trust and know that there is healing power in the Name of Jesus. Touch the body that's withered up with arthritis and help them to be able to walk or stand more briskly today than they did yesterday. Touch the cancer stricken and give them the strength they need to endure their chemo and or radiation to deaden all those cancer cells. Lord, touch those with chronic illness such as lupus, thyroidism, hypertension and diabetes so they can push through the weakness, push through the weight gain, push past the aching muscles and make it through the day with a smile and an increased sense of endurance.

Please touch the minds of those struggling with mental and emotional illness. Stop the noise they hear, the racing heartbeats they experience and Lord, subdue the roller coaster mood swings. Give them a settled spirit and a calmer demeanor so they can sort through their feelings. Lord, open their ears so they can hear Your word. Please, focus their eyes on positive things and give them pure and

spiritual filled thoughts to ease their
troubled minds.
Lord, we know that all sickness isn't a death sentence
and for that we say thank You. In Jesus Name,
Amen

Do not grieve, for the joy of the lord is your strength. Isaiah 41:10

Dear Lord,

Thank You for today. Thank You for all things great and small. Being able to say thank You for life during this season of global pandemic has an extra special meaning.

Lord, you have brought us through seen and unseen dangers and carried us through so many uncharted waters. You have brought us through mess we manufactured and then tried to sell off as someone else's mess.

Through, meaning to pass in one side and go out the other side. Thank You for not letting us get stuck in that desert experience. While we were "going through", You didn't allow us to die in our dark and lonely place, thank You Lord. As a matter of fact, some of us were able to find strengths we never knew we had spring forth like an oasis as we languished in our barren place of "through". The strength to hold on to our faith when darkness was all around us, the strength to speak Your Name when no other name could help and the courage to keep passing through our go through even as new road blocks, obstacles and challenges came our way.

Through our desert experiences we dealt with

seasons of drought and despair, but once we reached the other side of through our oasis of blessings awaited us. Through Your death, we gained life and through accepting You in our life, we gained access to the Kingdom. Lord, You died so we could live and through Your death we received eternal life. Thank You for loving us through our sinful periods and through our disobedience. We say thank You because now we realize we must go through to have completion of our journey. Lord, through You we are blessed beyond measure. Thanking You for our go through experiences and praising You for allowing through to be a process in which we not only overcome, but we grow.

In Jesus Name,

Amen

Rejoice in hope, be patient in tribulation, be constant in prayer. -Romans 12:12

Good Morning Lord!
Thank You for this day and last night's rest filled sleep. Thank You for waking me this morning with a renewed sense of energy and a spirit of readiness. Today we come asking for peace of mind. So many of us are struggling right now with an overload of things we are dealing with. Many of us are nearing a stage of burnout and the weights we are carrying aren't necessarily ours. Lord, so many of us have to listen and be available for our family, friends and even strangers as they pour their souls out to us and expect us to encourage and support them. Right now, Lord I come asking You to embrace those who are heavy laden from carrying others challenges and give them a sense of relief.

Lord, help them to speak victory over the feeling of defeat and despair, give them a boost of divine energy so their shoulders and hearts won't be so heavy from carrying others loads. Lord, help those who are weary, give them the strength they need just to speak Your Name.

Lord, we know if we can just call upon Your Name, speak an encouraging word from Your Word things will get better. Lord, let us speak Your name as we minister to ourselves in order to be lifted from these dark and heavy places, we find our hearts resting. Help us to speak Your name, the name above all names. The name that we speak to be saved, healed, comforted, and protected. The name above all Names!

Father God, as You give us strength to do so, we know things will work out. Thanking You in advance for the will power to speak victory over myself, others to speak victory over themselves and to speak deliverance from the demons around us. Lord, I speak Your name speak for healing into the atmosphere, I speak Your name over myself for an encouraging word so I can continue to live so people can see the Christ in me.

Thank You Lord for Your love which lifts us, Your goodness which guides us, Your strength which supports us and Your power which protects us. Yes, sometimes we do have to encourage ourselves, but it's so much easier knowing Gods got us covered and His Word and His Will keep us encouraged at all times. We love you Lord.
In Jesus Name,
Amen.

Therefore, do not worry about tomorrow, for tomorrow will worry about itself; each day has enough trouble of its own. -Matthew 6:34

Dear Lord,
Thank You for today. Lord yesterday was a challenge for some of us, yet we made it and we want to say thank You for bringing us to today. We love You Lord.

Lord, we are living in such a precarious time. The coronavirus is spreading like wildfire, government officials and egocentric politicians are creating false narratives, gun violence is at epidemic rates in our inner cities, yet we are all still trying to hold on and do the best we can. Lord, You are the only real constant in our lives and truly You are the only real answer to all of the mayhem and dysfunction.

The stresses of everyday life can wear us down and cause us to get weary sometimes. It was never promised to us that this life would be easy, but we never expected some of the lofty weights we have to carry. However, there is a blessing in knowing You walk with us and You help carry every heavy load we have or will have. Thank you for the strength to hold on to our faith when despair is all around us. Lord we say thank You for the strength to whisper Your Name above all the noise and the courage to keep holding on to Your unchanging hand, no matter what situation we are dealing with.

Thank You, for reminding us to hold onto Your Word while we walk through these valleys and side roads of mayhem and dysfunction. Your word fortifies us and gives us the strength we need to press on. Lord, it's Your word that uplifts our spirits and changes our moods when we are feeling the weight of this world on our shoulders. We are grateful we can "look to the hills from whence cometh our help" and we can be reminded that "God so loved the world He gave His only begotten Son that whom so ever believe in Him shall not perish but have everlasting life". Your word encourages us, it uplifts us and it fuels our souls.

Lord, right now we come asking that You be a fence around Your children, protect us from stray bullets, and alleviate our anxiety while being inundated by mistruth on top of mistruth by our government and political leadership. Please dear Lord, let us find comfort, direction and a sense of authority to change things and correct things according to Your word as we move in Your will.

Yesterday, gone but not forgotten, today, another chance to get things right and tomorrow our opportunity to reflect back on yesterday and today and do better. Tomorrow is not promised and that is why all of our today's matter. Lord help us so we can be grounded in our faith today, led by Your word today and share it with love today. Let us relinquish yesterday for there are no do overs. Let us treasure today as tomorrow May not come; and let us trust that if tomorrow comes we will be ever so thankful to see it!

We thank You for Your Word, Your Way and Your Wonder!
In Jesus Name

In peace I will lie down and sleep for you alone, O Lord, will keep me safe. - Psalm 4:8

Dear Father,
Here I am again on this early morning You have kept me. It's in these early morning hours I spend my best one-on-one time with You. It's been such a daunting and challenging time, yet in the midst of all this I find myself at peace. Thank You Lord.

People are confined to their homes, some are separated from loved ones, others can't celebrate with family and friends as we all are doing our part to be socially distanced. I come to You right now asking that You step in and adjust the levels of anxiety and stress some are dealing with at this time. Lord we are asking that the spirit of anxiousness be removed and replaced with an uplifted spirit of great expectation. We know that anxiousness sets in heavy due to uncertainty, rumors, dealing with the unknown and simply being isolated from others. Lord we are asking that you lift the weight of darkness and anxiety from those who are struggling and suffering. Yes, we know that You are the Light of the World and there is nothing that You do not control.

Stop all wandering thoughts that are stressing us out, tame the tricks of the heart and mind causing us to feel afraid, alone, and anxious. Then we ask that You replace the feelings of depression, disconnection, and despair with an increased sense of faith, that no matter what's going on today or tomorrow, You are in total control, so we will be alright. We ask that You breathe a fresh anointing of life, love, laughter, and contentment over those who are struggling.

Be with the family members and loved ones who surround those who are dealing with anxiety and stress. Please, give them the words they need to encourage and support their loved ones. Lord, let them be patient and compassionate as they assist their loved ones in dealing with anxiety and mood swings. Help them so they can find solace and comfort in Your words and peace of mind through Your love.

Thanking You Lord for lifting the heavy weight and easing the rapid rush of anxiety, and letting peace take hold of our minds and hearts. God, You are a healer and a help, and we cry out to You to heal us and help us to return to a healthy and hopeful state of mind.

Thanking You in advance for restored joy, renewed peace of mind and a calm and reinvigorated spirit. We love You Lord and we thank You for settling our stress and alleviating our anxiety. You alone are worthy of our praise.
In Your precious name,
Amen

You shall not murder-Exodus 20:13

Dear Lord,
Thank You for bringing us to this day. There is so much turmoil in our land.

Lord today we are praying for unity in our families, justice in our communities and peace in our country. Lord we ask that You cover us with Your powerful hand.

Help us to realize diversity is our strength. Lord help us to realize unity and justice are not based on our skin tone, our race, our ethnicity, or our gender, but based on respect, understanding, human decency, pure kindness, and true brotherly/sisterly love. Help us to realize love ALWAYS wins.

Lord give us the spirit of humility so we can share our ideas and opinions with each other without fear or intimidation. Help us to peel back the layers of generations of subservient attitudes, supremacy and ignorance regarding each other's cultures and backgrounds. Lord, open jaded eyes so they can see the human spirit and not the skin color. Replace hardened and hateful hearts with understanding and unified mindsets.

It's a very scary and painful time when black men are fearful of the police killing them over a traffic stop, falling asleep in their car or placing a knee on their neck until they die. Then our black men must be fearful of white neighbors killing them for jogging in the neighborhood or calling the police on them for bird watching, and young black men killing each other almost as a sport. What have we become as a society?

Lord, we need You to be a hedge of protection around our young men of color. We need You to pierce the hearts of those who see a darker skin tone as an invitation to mistreatment and even death. You are the only one who can cleanse this land of racism, hatred, and ignorance. Please keep us covered as we attempt to educate others about diversity, model good decent behavior and speak up and speak out against any and every type of hatred and evil.

Lord, help us to stand firm on the foundations of truth, respect and honor and not give in to the tenets of bigotry, hatred, and deceit. Thank You for those who choose to stand up against injustice and try to unify people with positive interaction.

Help us all to remember we were ALL created in Your image, we were ALL created by You and we ALL have been instructed to live in Your will, love others as You love us and show respect to each other as we reverence You.

We love You Lord and we thank You in advance for the healing that is going to take place in this fractured and fickle world we live in. Help us Lord! Only as You can!! In Jesus name, Amen

Do not grieve, for the joy of the Lord is your strength- Nehemiah 8:10

Dear Lord,

Thank You for one more day. Thank You for keeping me.

Today I come on behalf of those struggling with addictions. There are so many things which grab a hold-of us as we try to navigate this thing called life. Lord, today I am interceding on behalf of those who are struggling with addictions to alcohol, drugs, sex, food, and social media. Lord, whatever it is that consumes their time, their minds, their attitudes and their actions that is not of You or through You, we come right now asking that we be delivered from what is binding us.

Lord, we know that we can fall prey to so many things in this world. We come asking for strength, direction and deliverance from these things which have become distractions, things that have caused harm to us. Lord, we are pleading with You to deliver us from things that create negative mindsets and become chains of bondage on our everyday existence. Help us to lean not to our own understanding but learn how to exercise our faith and lean and depend on You.

I come today asking that chains of addiction can begin to be broken for people and deliverance from the "thing" that holds them captive will surely come. Lord, we are praying for strength to withstand the temptation to fall into an addictive state, knowledge to remain free and perseverance to keep moving forward. Dear Father, help those who are struggling with addiction to be able to accept the things they cannot change. Let them have enough faith and courage to trust You and seek deliverance from the stronghold of whatever their addiction might be.

Lord, please deliver us from our obsessive and addictive behaviors. Deliver us from being weak in our flesh and give us positive power through our prayers so we can overcome our addictions. We are thanking You right now for the victory in letting alcohol go, being released from the chains of gambling, drug use and yes even overeating.

Thank You in advance for delivering us, releasing us, and empowering us to let that addiction go. Glory to Your Name, Amen

When the righteous cry for help, the Lord hears and delivers them out of all their troubles- Psalm 34:17

Dear Lord,
Thank you for another day You have blessed us to see. We are indeed grateful!

Lord today we come just to say "Please". Please help us Lord. Our country is fractured, she is broken, and we need You! Please!!

Lord, we have families who are currently preparing to lay their loved ones to rest, who were taken by violence at the hands of each other and some at the hands of the police. Lord, for those families we say, "Please" provide comfort during their time of grief. Please provide understanding as to why a trip to the store led to an evil act of hatred. Please!!!

We have family and friends dealing with terminal illness and having to watch their loved ones suffer from cancer, strokes, and other diseases. We come asking that You "Please" give those afflicted with these illnesses the strength they need to endure, let their faith become the weapon they use to fight on. "Please" let them feel the love and prayers of those supporting them.

Lord, "Please ", be with the family members who have to be caregivers and those who must make life altering decisions. "Please" help them to lean not to their own understanding but to wholly lean and depend on you! "Please" boost their faith during these trying times and "Please" help us all to remember that

You are in control and You never fail.
"Please" reign down on us with Your mercy and Your grace and prepare our hearts and minds so we can handle whatever lies ahead that's of Your will and way!"

"Please", heal our land; please restore civility and compassion back into our communities. "Please", Lord tame the deceitful, dishonest, disingenuous, and disgusting words and actions that are being lobbied about. Lord, "Please" help us eradicate the vile and evil systemic racism that this country was built on and still struggles with.

We need Thee, oh we need Thee. "Please" hear our please! Please Lord, save us from ourselves and "Please", heal this hurting land.

"Please" bless our going and coming as we navigate what today might hold.
In Jesus Name,
Amen!

The Lord is good, a refuge in times of trouble. He cares for those who trust in him. Nahum 1:7

Dear Lord,

Thank You Lord for one more day and another opportunity to say Thank You. Lord, we are truly living in a time of trouble. There is so much violence, corruption, and just evil deeds all around us. The chaos clatters so loudly that it causes us to wonder is there any good left in our world. Lord, today we come crying out to You, for You alone can be our present help in these times of trouble. Lord, we know as Christians we aren't exempt from trouble and we aren't immune to having trouble visit us. Dear Lord, trouble comes in so many ways and sometimes it blindsides us to the point of despair.

There's trouble in our land due to racism, sexism, and social economic disparity. Trouble with people killing each other almost as a sport, trouble, Lord we are surrounded by trouble!! Lord, we need Your loving and gracious touch in so many different places right now. We need You to- touch the hearts of our political leaders and help them to turn to You, Your will and Your way for direction and guidance. Help them to stop being such ego driven, nonfunctioning and self- engrossed people and get back to having a true heart for service, a heart for helping and a heart for the least of them.

We come today, asking for Your presence in our time of trouble, for peace to overtake the violence and turmoil in our midst and for Your power to give us the strength we as children of God need to stand boldly for what's right and fight to make things better. Lord we are calling on You to steer us in the right direction away for the chaos and trouble and back down avenues filled with tranquility and togetherness. Our prayer today is extremely specific Lord, let us put these guns down and pick up our Bibles, let us stop all the racist and sexist rhetoric and replace it with talks of harmony and understanding each other's differences. Lord, we are in need of Your persistent power right now to turn things around. We know that trouble doesn't last always, and we are very grateful that You already know the outcome. There is power in prayer and we thank God for that.

In Jesus Name, Amen

Now may the Lord of peace himself give you peace at all times and in every way. The Lord be with you. - 2Thessalonians 3:16

Dear Lord,
Thank You Lord for this day and for Your continued showers of grace and mercy. We count ever blessing as a bonus   from You.

Lord, today we come asking for tolerance. We are living in such a precarious time where things are in a chaotic state. The time for understanding each other, understanding our differences, and understanding how to live in peace and harmony is at hand.

Please help us to be more tolerant of those who don't look like us and who don't speak our language. Help us to always remember we are all God's children and we are all unique and divinely created by You. Lord, give us an open mind, so we can use our diversity as strength instead of a hindrance. Let our mindset be one off inclusion, not exclusion and one of helping not hate.

Lord, adjust our attitudes so we can remain compassionate towards all races, all genders, all ethnic groups, and all people. Let us exhibit equality in all of our actions and interactions with people who are not like us. Pour into us a spirit of sisterhood/brotherhood that is so powerful people will recognize it without delay.

We are all Your children and we all need You right now, Father God in a mighty way. Let our tongues be coated in care, concern and compassion and let our eyes be filled with vision unity and togetherness Thank You for showing us that there is great hope, greater expectation and even greater joy in understanding and being tolerant of each other.

In Jesus Name,

Amen

Love the Lord your God and keep his requirements, his decrees, his laws, and his commands always. -Deuteronomy 11:1

Dear Lord,
Good Morning. You granted us one more day......thank You. Lord, there is so much going on around us which causes us to be anxious and even short tempered with each other. Today, we come asking that You will not only give us peace of mind, but Lord; we are also asking that You give us a mindset which is filled with obedience to Your Word, Your will and Your way.

Lord, we want to be obedient in our service to You, in our actions and in our thoughts. We realize that a life which is lived to please You is one where we follow all of the Commandments You have given us without any wavering. Now, we also understand that due to our human nature we will make mistakes and do things which are not pleasing to You, but we thank God for forgiveness. Through Your shed blood we received another chance at life and redemption. Thank You God, for sacrificing Your   Son, so we could live.

Today, we come to with clean hearts, clear minds, calm spirits, and compassionate tongues, ready to be about the right thing and to be obedient to the Word and will of God. Lord, adjust our attitudes and let our lives become walking billboards for who and what we can be once we submit to following You and living a life of obedience.

Thank You for loving us enough to give us guidelines and commandments in order to live a life that is pleasing in Your sight. We know that obedience is better than sacrifice and obedience leads to rewards from You.

We love You Lord and we are so grateful for all You have done, are doing and will do. In Jesus Name, Amen

So, God created man in his own image, in the image of God he created him. -Genesis 1:27

Dear Lord,
Thank You for a brand-new day You blessed us to see. Thank You for being such a gracious and loving Father.

Today, we come asking for a new awakening of human kindness and decency in our land. Lord, help us to get back to speaking to our neighbors and getting to know them, versus cursing them. Shakeup our moral compass and allow us to get back on the path of being moral and upright in our dealings with one another. Please bring us back to a place where civility, compassion and courtesy are the norm and not the exception. Lord, lead us and guide us so we can not only embrace brotherly love, but we can live it and model it for others to experience and see in action. We come right now asking for a divine touch over this country. Where there is racial discord, give us the tools we need to bring about true equality and learn to appreciate diversity. Where there is economic and social disparity, help us find a way to make access to resources fairer and more attainable.

America needs a revival of its true spirit of being a country whose motto is "In God We Trust". Open our eyes so we can be aware of the egocentric, narcissistic and self- indulged politicians and leaders who don't have anyone's interest at heart except theirs. Let us have an awakening of our spirit so we will get back to standing up for the right things and not kneeling down to worship any idols, but only worship You.

Breathe a fresh wind of absolute resolution over us today Lord, so we can turn things around before it is too late. Fix our minds, adjust our ability to reason properly and give us strength to stand on Your Word, not mans!

"God bless America, land that we love
Stand beside her and guide her
Through the night with the light from above.
God bless America, our home sweet home."
Please Lord, in Your Name we pray,
Amen!

Trust in the Lord and do good; dwell in the land and enjoy safe pasture. -Psalm 37:3

Dear Lord,
On today we just want to say, "We trust You Lord!" We trust You to safely guide us through the process of facing life's challenges. We trust You to give us the strength we need to endure the tests which lie ahead. We trust You Lord; we know you will never leave us nor forsake us! We trust You to be our buffer as we deal with various storms and trials.

Lord, we trust that You will be our light in darkness, our quiet place in the midst of chaos and our wiper blades when torrential storms come, clearing our view to s e e what is ahead of us!
Lord, we trust You because we know what You have done, can do and that You are in control. Yes, we trust You because You loved us enough to give us the ultimate sacrifice, so we could live! We trust You because You are our amazing grace and our solid rock.
In Jesus Name,
 Amen.

Have pity upon me, have pity upon me. O, ye my friends; for the hand of God hath touched me. Job 19:21

Dear Lord,

Thank You for a good night's rest and an early morning wake-up! Once again, we are blessed to see a new day!

There are many who are struggling with depression, loneliness, and isolation during this time. Today we come Lord, asking that You will touch their minds and give them clarity. Lord, help them to be able to sort through their thoughts and find some sense of peace and security. Let them be reminded that You are their Heavenly Father and You are always with them.

Adjust their attitudes so they can choose laughter over lamenting, hope over helplessness, self-love over self-loathing and determination over depression. Lord, open their ears so they can hear Your word which can and will sustain them. Let them find comfort in knowing You are a mind regulator, heart fixer and an attitude adjuster.

Lord, give the loved ones, family, and friends of those struggling with depression the right words to speak and the insight to know when to simply be still and let God handle the situation.

We come asking that You will blow a fresh wind of

peace over their lives so chaos can be limited, blow a fresh wind of emotional strength over them so they will not succumb to depression. Lord, spark a fire in their soul and let it burn with encouragement and enlightenment.

Thank You for being a healer of our mind, a filter for our emotions and a keeper of our spirit. We love You Lord for lifting us from dark places and for elevating our attitudes to a new and intensified level in You. Thank You for the emotional breakthroughs, healings, and spiritual restorations You are about to manifest in us!!
In Jesus Name, Amen

But all things should be done decent and in order.
- 1 Corinthians 14:40

Dear Heavenly Father,
Thank You for this day, Your loving protection, and Your loving kindness. Lord, we love You with our whole heart.

We come today seeking peace of mind, a settling of our spirits and healing of a land that's filled with chaos, untruths, and confusion. Today we are all one click away from losing our sanity whether it's over the coronavirus19, the failing stock market, rampant gun violence in our inner cities or drug abuse. Lord, we are coming right now asking for a spiritual awaking, a divinely inspired intervention and a powerful hedge of protection for all Your children.

We come today seeking Your guidance as this world is dealing with a medical pandemic, Covid19, sweeping from country to country, leaving behind death, devastation and financial decay. Only You, God can protect and heal our land. As this medical plague rolls from one continent to the next, let this be one a humbling experience for those who think they can make it without You in their lives. Lord, please protect us from the deadly virus as well as the corruption and disintegration of a healthy and holy society. Let us try to find our way back to You, by turning from our sinful and wicked ways.

Help us to get back to a place-where we respect one another, work cooperatively with others and worship You in spirit and total truth. Lord, help us to stop using religion and our relationship with You as some type of qualifier for elite status in today's world. Lord please prick the hearts of those in leadership who are messing with people's livelihoods and let them get back to being led by Your laws, Your love and You leading us daily.

Lord, we need a touch from You to end this pandemic, stop all this gun violence and curb our sinful nature. Help us to turn from these wicked and hateful ways and restore accountability, respect, love, and decency back into our society. Lord, we know You hold the cure in Your hand, we know You can stop the violence with Your hands lifted high and yes, we know You are taking care of things as we pray and we are very grateful.

As I close my mind reflects back to numerous stories in Your word, the Bible, which describes mayhem, dysfunction and separation. Lord, we don't want to be separated from You, Your word, or Your way. Please Dear Lord, heal our land and restore us back to a sacred sweet and nurturing relationship with You, especially in times of chaos and dysfunction.
In Jesus Name,
Amen

God said to Moses, I am Who I am. Exodus 3:14

Lord,

On today we come simply to say thank You! Thank You for waking us up this morning and starting us on our way. We are so grateful that You allowed Your hand of protection to cover us.

Over the course of this past two months during the pandemic, there have been situations which have occurred that could have had bad outcomes, but God You, stepped in! We are so grateful Lord for Your hands of protection and provision. Through storms and challenging times, we stand still knowing You are God. It gives us great comfort because we are reminded that You are in control.

Please keep our minds stayed on You, our hearts open to receive Your word to hide in our hearts and our focus on things above and not below. Lord, please keep our hands tightly clasped to Your will and our feet solidly walking in Your way. As we saturate our minds with Your word, keep our hearts pure and clean and our actions filled with love and compassion.

Today we just want to say thank You for being our strong tower and our guiding light. We love You Lord and we are grateful for ALL of our blessings, seen and unseen. Thank You for being in control of all things, everything and even in control of things we consider to be nothing! As stated in Your word, "I am that I am", You are our all and all and our all in all. Thank You Lord.In Jesus Name, Amen

These trials will show that your faith is geniune.1 Peter 1:7

Dear Lord,
Hello Lord and thank You for one more day. Thank You for Your loving kindness towards us.

Lord, as we stand at the crossroads of life, we face challenges and deal with situations on a daily basis. Right now, we want to talk about the tests along our way.

Lord, thank You for drying the tears we shed while dealing with tragedies that tested our faith. Thank You for being a fence all around us when we were dealing with the test of our enemies trying to tempt us and draw us into evil places. Thank You for bringing the calming words of Blessed Assurance to mind when our patience was tested by having to deal with a frustrating situation. Lord, thank You for holding our tongue so we would speak Gods word and not worldly words against the person who was trying to cause us to "snap".

In life we must study, to pass the tests that we find ourselves facing. As we study Your Word and remain prayerful, we become better equipped to handle tests along our journey. Thank You for the instruction manual You gave us in the Bible. Lord, thank You for the examples of how to live and deal with our trials You showed us through Your life.

Lord, once we have conquered our tests, we can share with others so they won't stumble over the same traps or fall prey to the same evil forces. Yes, it is only a test and as long as we stay fed through Your Word, covered by Your grace, and protected by our prayers- we can handle and even pass the tests that life sends our way. It's only a test that you are going through. Remember our God has His hand all over you! It is only a test!
In Jesus Name,
Amen

The Lord is my Shepherd; I shall not want-Psalm 23:1

Dear Lord,
Thank You for this morning, which is another day I didn't deserve, but one You have allowed me to see. You are such an amazing and marvelous Father to all of us, thank You Lord.

Today I am so grateful for You allowing me to be living in my overflow. I am not materially wealthy, but rich in all the ways which matter. Thank You Lord, for my overflow, my parents who taught me about prayer and the importance of having a relationship with You. Thank You for my husband, a man who loves, serves, and honors You, as well as loves and provides for me. Lord, we are grateful for our children who acknowledge and worship You and our grandchildren who are covered and protected by You.

Thank You for my overflow, not perfect health, but I am not bed ridden or hospital bound. I am alive, breathing and moving all my limbs, with my mind intact, my thoughts and conversations make sense and I know who I am. Lord thank You for my overflow, my supportive and loving family, a loving and caring extended family, a loyal circle of friends and a great church home.

Thank You for my overflow, no weapons formed against me prospering, no matter how they try to

attack, no demons tricking me and my enemies can't block my path.
Thank You for my overflow..... my cup is never 1/2 empty, but always 1/2 full. Thank You for my praying mother, my devoted father and all my ancestors who knew You, served You and passed along the importance of loving You and walking in Your will and way to the next generation.

Thank You for my overflow!!!
In Jesus Name,
Amen.

The Lord is with me; I will not be afraid. What can mere mortals do? - Psalm118:6

Good Morning Lord,
Lord, we simply stopped by this morning to say thank You! It is another day You have granted us which provides us another opportunity to praise Your name and be of service to someone along the way. Thank You.

Lord, as we look back on our week, we realize You have kept us from hurt, harm and danger. You provided all our needs, calmed our sorrows, and relieved our fears. You provided for us before we had to ask and, in many cases, You blessed us beyond measure. Lord, thank You.

Today is a good day because You kept us, You blessed us, and You showed us mercy and grace. When we stumbled, You caught us, when we fell You picked us up, when we were lost, You found us and when we hurt, You soothed us.

You are the beginning and You are the end. You and You alone have every answer to all our questions. Thank You for breathing life into us and allowing us an opportunity to call You, our Father.

*We love You; we praise You and we thank You. It's
Sunday morning and we are so blessed that our
Father, which is in heaven continues to rule, reign,
and reside over us and with us! Thank You Lord, for
being so good.*
*Lord we say Thank You and we are so grateful for
one more day.*
In Jesus Name,
Amen

REFLECTION

In times of turmoil, chaos and confusion how do you connect with God?

____

____

____

____

____

____

____

List the scriptures you read to settle a troubled spirit. How did you decide these were the ones to use?

____

____

____

How have you been dealing with the anxiety that is caused by all the racial unrest? Are you leaning more on your faith and praying more often?

____

____

____

____

____

____

Has your prayer life gotten stronger during times of pandemic and trouble? Why do you think that is the case?

____

____

____

____

Do you believe God is in the midst of these strange times? What do you think He is speaking to your heart?

____

____

____

____

How has your faith sustained you during times of racial discord?

____

____

____

____

____

____

____

____

____

How can you use your faith to ease injustice in our society?

For whosoever shall call upon the name of the Lord shall be saved. -Romans 10:13

Dear Lord,

There is a name that is so special and very dear to me. Jesus is the sweetest name I know. Lord, thank You for this opportunity where I can just talk to You and pour out my soul.

Looking back over my life I have been blessed to make it pass death knocking at my door, loved ones transitioning, health issues, financial uncertainty and so many other challenges, Lord, I want to pause to say thank You. Thank You for the multitude of blessings you have bestowed upon me. I am not and have not always been worthy, but You showed mercy on me and I say thank You.

As I travel down Blessings Blvd., I am reminded of your unending goodness. I am so grateful that I have been able to cross over onto Loving Lane, as You loved us so much, You died so we could live. In my latter years I have been fortunate to walk down Wisdom Way as I have grown in my knowledge of your word, giving me greater insights into my everyday living. Then You allowed me to turn the corner and stroll up Compassionate Court to check on those who cannot always help themselves. Once I walked down Servant Street after helping those in need, I got to Rest-a-Little-While Road, where I sat down and reflected.

Lord, thank You for Your goodness, grace, love, sacrifice and for giving me one more chance, even when I don't deserve it. I love You and I am incredibly grateful for all You have done and are doing.
In Jesus Name, Amen

So, faith comes from hearing and hearing through the word of Christ- Romans 10:17

Dear Lord,
Early in the morning as I rise, I lift my eyes to the hills, for all my help comes from Thee! Another night of storms rolled through and You kept us safe! Thank You Lord.

Lord, sometimes we let other people's problems and situations impact our attitude and our faith. Today, I come asking that You would strengthen our resolve so we can stand strong in and on our faith. Help us so we won't become skeptical or cynical about our faith when we see or hear others who are dealing with life's challenges and they don't know You.

Lord, help us to find a way to let Your love shine through us so others might recognize there's something different about us. Help us as believers to stop being timid and ashamed to let people know that living for You, serving You and trusting You makes all the difference. It truly does payoff.

Lord, it's hard to express sometimes, but You are my everything and I do love You. I ask for forgiveness where I fall short and I ask for guidance so I will do better.

I will keep looking to the hills from whence cometh my help! I am grateful that You never sleep or slumber, therefore I never need to fear that You don't know my needs! I am so grateful that You are omnipresent (always present), omnipotent (all powerful) and omniscient (all knowing).
So thankful to know who Jesus is and to truly know that You are real in my life.
In a Jesus Name, Amen

Be still and know that I am God. I am exalted among the nations; I will be exalted in the earth. - Psalm 46:10

It's another beautiful morning because we are still here! Thank You for waking me up and letting me see this day.

Today we come praying for those who have lost their hope! Those whose sense of anticipation and expectation is waning! Those who are often found looking at their past because they are afraid to look forward. Lord, today we come asking that You restore and renew their hope!

We know that faith is confidence or trust in a belief or a person, and as Christians we know that faith is the substance of things hoped for and the evidence of things unseen. Lord, we also realize that hope is an optimistic mindset or attitude towards something! Lord, through Your word and living a life for You we come asking for Increased sense of hope/expectation that our circumstances will improve and our daily walk with bring us closer to You!

Strengthen our resolve so we can stand firmly planted on Your word, knowing that as long as we can have hope in You, hope in a better life through the gift of salvation and hope for a better tomorrow by leaning and depending on You, everything will be alright.

Lord, help us to put our faith in You so we can hope for things in high and mighty places! Let our level of expectation and our desires be for things which are healthy, helpful and will not harm or hinder us!

Please elevate our hope which is a desire to please you! Lord, restore our hope - an expectation of goodness and greatness in our lives! Lastly, Lord please increase our hope for things that are of You, directed by You and through You, so we can leave our fears and doubts in the distant past.

We are thanking You right now for truly we want to be able to proclaim that our hope is built on nothing less than Jesus and all of His righteousness. Thank You for reminding us that faith the size of a mustard seed can move a mountain and the very whispering of the word hope can brighten our day!
In Jesus Name,
Amen

Watch and pray that you may not enter into temptation. The spirit indeed is willing, but the flesh is weak. Matthew 26:41

Good Morning Lord,
It's me again just being grateful that You never get tired of hearing from me or any of your children.
I am so blessed to be able to live my life out loud and on purpose. I want to say thank You for giving me the words I need to use to talk to You and share my thoughts and my needs. Thank You for being the answer to every question, the comma when I need to pause and take a break and the exclamation point on all my victories. Thank You Lord!!

I come now thanking You for the burning passion I have to live on purpose while serving my purpose. Thank You for the prayers and our one on one time with each other. I have grown in grace, grown in my walk and, most of all I am a bolder witness about You and Your goodness. I am a walking billboard and I am not ashamed.

Lord, I am grateful for Your guiding light which directs my path and causes me to stay focused even when I have become my greatest distraction. Lord, I am living my best life for You, through You and because of You I can live.

Thank You for allowing me to breathe, move and have my mind so I can continue to live and love with a passion that exemplifies my purpose, while living out loud proclaiming that You are indeed Lord of my life. My prayers have sustained me, changed me, matured me, molded me, and defined my purpose in this life. Thank you for my prayers, my purpose, and Your

promise. I love You Lord, I do.
In Jesus name,
Amen.